YOUR BEST FRIEND ~~WON'T TELL~~
YOU . . .

. . . if you make embarrassing errors in spelling, grammar, or pronunciation—but the self-testing exercises in this book will. Discover your areas of weakness with over one hundred revealing and informative quizzes on vocabulary and usage, such as—

1) What's the difference between *who* and *whom*?
2) Which is correct: *recommend* or *reccommend*?
3) Do *taciturn* and *loquacious* mean the same or opposite?
4) True or false: After *between*, use only objective pronouns—*me, him, her, us, them.*

If you're not absolutely sure of your answers, try

# THIRTY DAYS TO BETTER ENGLISH

. . . and teach yourself to "express for success"!

NORMAN LEWIS is a noted teacher, editor and author. His previous books include THIRTY DAYS TO A MORE POWERFUL VOCABULARY, HOW TO READ BETTER & FASTER, and INSTANT WORD POWER (available in a Signet edition).

1) *Who* is the subject of a verb; *whom* is its object.
2) *Recommend* 3) Opposite. 4) True.

# THIRTY DAYS TO BETTER ENGLISH

by Norman Lewis

A SIGNET BOOK

NEW AMERICAN LIBRARY

Published by arrangement with the author.

**Library of Congress Catalog Card Number: 84-62277**

SIGNET TRADEMARK REG. U.S. PAT. OFF. AND FOREIGN COUNTRIES
REGISTERED TRADEMARK—MARCA REGISTRADA
HECHO EN CHICAGO, U.S.A.

SIGNET, SIGNET CLASSIC, MENTOR, ONYX, PLUME, MERIDIAN
and NAL BOOKS are published by NAL PENGUIN INC.,
1633 Broadway, New York, New York 10019

First Signet Printing, April, 1985

2  3   4   5   6   7   8   9   10

PRINTED IN THE UNITED STATES OF AMERICA

for
Mary, Margie, Debbie

# *Contents*

### PART I. TEST YOUR ENGLISH!

# PART II. SAY IT RIGHT!

Your reaction to nine significant English words will tell you a great deal about your pronunciation habits.

Here are 25 important words that poor speakers say in a slovenly fashion. How about you?

You complete your understanding of the principles of correct pronunciation by examining four final categories of English words; then you check the success of your learning in Part II by taking a pronunciation test that most unsophisticated speakers would do very poorly on.

# PART III. IMPROVE YOUR VOCABULARY!

To increase your vocabulary at a prodigious rate, you must learn to be on the alert for new words.

If you work from Latin and Greek roots you can add new words to your vocabulary in wholesale quantities!

A quick warm-up that will help you add some short and expressive terms to your vocabulary.

## PART V. SPEAK CORRECTLY!

Let's find out if your everyday English is as good as you are.

No other verbs cause as much trouble as *lay* and *lie*. Now you can begin mastering them by learning a few simple and easy-to-apply principles.

Today you nail down your understanding of these troublesome verbs and prove to yourself that you can now avoid all confusion.

Do you have to stop sometimes and wonder whether to use *is* or *are, has* or *have, was* or *were*? Let's discover how easy it is to decide once you're sure of the rules.

## PART VI. THE MODERN VIEW OF CORRECTNESS IN ENGLISH

An informal investigation for *Harper's Magazine* that turned up some surprising results.

# PART I

# *Test Your English!*

*Do you make embarrassing errors in pronunciation, spelling, grammar, word usage?*

*Is your vocabulary fresh and growing, or do you use the same old tired words over and over?*

*In short, does your English work for you or against you?*

## HERE'S YOUR CHANCE TO FIND OUT!

The words you use can either work for you or against you—and, in a very real sense, you are the one who chooses which it's to be.

For, rightly or wrongly, you are often judged not only by what you say but, more immediately, by how you say it. Your language, whether in speech or writing, announces to the world—to your friends, to your business or professional associates, indeed to everyone with whom you come in contact for no matter how brief a time—*this is the kind of person I am.*

The relationships you have with other people are largely dependent on words—you communicate to others your feelings, your needs, your ideas, your reactions in words. *More important, you continuously present yourself in words.*

Just what kind of person do others see when you

translate your thoughts into speech or writing? Part I will help you find out—will help you discover what your spelling, pronunciation, and grammar say about you.

# First Day

## TEST YOUR PRONUNCIATION

---

Four short, but revealing, pronunciation tests give you an accurate indication of how you sound to other people.

---

### DOES YOUR PRONUNCIATION HELP YOU PUT YOUR BEST FOOT FORWARD?

In the following four tests, check in each instance the pronunciation you naturally and habitually use—do not be influenced by what you think may or may not be "correct."

[The symbol ə indicates the very slight vowel sound heard in the first syllable of *commit* (kə-MIT′) or the last syllable of *Linda* (LIN′-də)].

**Test 1:** *Do You Avoid Common but Glaring Errors?*

If so, you will check the preferable pronunciation of at least four of the following five words.

| FOR: | DO YOU USUALLY SAY: |
|------|---------------------|
| 1. Italian | (a) ə-TAL'-yən, *or* |
|  | (b) eye-TAL'-yən? |
| 2. genuine | (a) JEN'-yoo-in, *or* |
|  | (b) JEN'-yoo-wine? |
| 3. theater | (a) thee-AY'-tər, *or* |
|  | (b) THEE'-ə-tər? |
| 4. nuclear | (a) NOO'-klee-ər, *or* |
|  | (b) NOO'-kyə-lər? |
| 5. pronunciation | (a) pro-NOUN'-see-ay-shən, *or* |
|  | (b) pro-NUN'-see-ay-shən? |

**How Did You Do?** *Check Your Results.*

1—a, 2—a, 3—b, 4—a, 5—b.

**Test 2:** *Does Your Pronunciation Meet Educated Standards?*

If so, you will check the preferred pronunciation of at least four of the following.

| FOR: | DO YOU USUALLY SAY: |
|------|---------------------|
| 1. percolator | (a) PUR'-kyoo-lay-tər, *or* |
|  | (b) PUR'-kə-lay-tər? |
| 2. preferable | (a) PREF'-ər-ə-bəl, *or* |
|  | (b) prə-FUR'-ə-bəl? |
| 3. phraseology | (a) fray-zee-OL'-ə-jee, *or* |
|  | (b) fray-ZOL'-ə-jee? |
| 4. extraordinary | (a) EX'-trə-OR'-də-ner-ee, *or* |
|  | (b) ex-TRAWR'-də-ner-ee? |
| 5. naïveté | (a) NAY'-və-tee, *or* |
|  | (b) nah-eev-TAY'? |

**How Did You Do?** *Check Your Results.*

1—b, 2—a, 3—a, 4—b, 5—b.

**Test 3:** *If You Use an Unknown Word, Do You Say It Correctly?*

If so, you will know the correct pronunciation of at least four of the following.

| FOR: | WOULD YOU SAY: |
|------|----------------|
| 1. epitome | (a) EP'-ǝ-tome, *or* (b) ǝ-PIT'-ǝ-mee? |
| 2. awry | (a) ǝ-RYE', *or* (b) AW'-ree? |
| 3. machinations | (a) match-ǝ-NAY'-shǝnz, *or* (b) mak-ǝ-NAY'-shǝnz? |
| 4. inexorable | (a) in-EX'-ǝr-ǝ-bǝl, *or* (b) IN'-ǝg-ZAWR'-ǝ-bǝl? |
| 5. ribald | (a) RYE'-bawld, *or* (b) RIB'-ǝld? |

**How Did You Do?** *Check Your Results.*

1–b, 2–a, 3–b, 4–a, 5–b.

**Test 4:** *Do You Ever Make People Uncomfortable with Affected Pronunciation?*

You probably don't—but check the preferable form in at least four of the following to be sure.

| FOR: | DO YOU GENERALLY SAY: |
|------|------------------------|
| 1. been | (a) BEAN, *or* (b) BIN? |
| 2. student | (a) STOO'-dǝnt, *or* (b) STYOO'-dǝnt? |
| 3. last | (a) LAHST, *or* (b) LAST? |
| 4. secretary | (a) SEK'-rǝ-tree, *or* (b) SEK'-rǝ-ter-ee? |
| 5. again | (a) ǝ-GEN', *or* (b) ǝ-GAYN'? |

**How Did You Do?** *Check Your Results.*

1–b, 2–a, 3–b, 4–b, 5–a.

# Second Day

## TEST YOUR VOCABULARY

---

React to 30 specially selected words to discover whether your vocabulary is *average, good,* or *superior.*

---

### DOES YOUR VOCABULARY REFLECT YOUR MENTAL STATURE?

It was discovered some years ago that one particular ability was common to all successful business executives. At the Human Engineering Laboratory, then affiliated with the Stevens Institute of Technology in New Jersey, aptitude tests were administered to thousands of adults from every walk of life. Without exception, the top names showed the greatest skill in just one field—*vocabulary.* And, again without exception, everyone who had an extensive vocabulary also held a high position in his chosen field.

Surprisingly, formal education turned out to have less relationship to the vocabulary score than might reasonably be expected. One man, a major executive of the telephone company, made a better showing than any of the college professors who had taken the tests. *And this man had left school at the age of 14!*

The three tests that follow will show you whether your vocabulary is average, good, or superior.

**Test 5:** *Do You Have an Average Vocabulary?*

If so, you will have no difficulty matching the two columns below. Seventy-five percent of the adults tested knew all these words.

| WORDS | MEANINGS |
|---|---|
| 1. imminent | (a) cleanse |
| 2. fluster | (b) flashy |
| 3. rigid | (c) confuse |
| 4. purge | (d) bring back to former excellence |
| 5. rehabilitate | (e) hinder |
| 6. latent | (f) pretend |
| 7. gaudy | (g) stiff |
| 8. feign | (h) coax |
| 9. cajole | (i) hidden |
| 10. impede | (j) likely to happen in the near future |

**How Did You Do?** *Check Your Results.*

1–j, 2–c, 3–g, 4–a, 5–d, 6–i, 7–b, 8–f, 9–h, 10–e.

**Test 6:** *Do You Have a Good Vocabulary?*

Decide whether words and meanings are *similar* or *opposite,* and check the correct box. Only 49 percent of the adults tested knew these words. You have a good vocabulary if you can get at least eight right.

| WORDS | MEANINGS | | |
|---|---|---|---|
| 1. myriad | small in number | SIMILAR ( ) | OPPOSITE ( ) |
| 2. panacea | cure-all | SIMILAR ( ) | OPPOSITE ( ) |

|  |  |  |  |
|---|---|---|---|
| 3. opulent | poverty-stricken | SIMILAR (  ) | OPPOSITE (  ) |
| 4. eschew | avoid | SIMILAR (  ) | OPPOSITE (  ) |
| 5. nefarious | wicked | SIMILAR (  ) | OPPOSITE (  ) |
| 6. incarcerate | imprison | SIMILAR (  ) | OPPOSITE (  ) |
| 7. ameliorate | make worse | SIMILAR (  ) | OPPOSITE (  ) |
| 8. candor | hypocrisy | SIMILAR (  ) | OPPOSITE (  ) |
| 9. taciturn | talkative | SIMILAR (  ) | OPPOSITE (  ) |
| 10. verbose | wordy | SIMILAR (  ) | OPPOSITE (  ) |

**How Did You Do?** *Check Your Results.*

1–OPPOSITE, 2–SIMILAR, 3–OPPOSITE, 4–SIMILAR, 5–SIMILAR, 6–SIMILAR, 7–OPPOSITE, 8–OPPOSITE, 9– OPPOSITE, 10–SIMILAR.

**Test 7:** *Do You Have a Superior Vocabulary?*

Determine which of the following statements are *true*, which *false*, and check the proper box. Only 22 percent of the adults tested knew these words, so yours is a superior vocabulary if you can react correctly to eight or more.

1. *Obsequiousness* is a sign of pride. TRUE (  ) FALSE (  )
2. *Parsimonious* people are extravagant. TRUE (  ) FALSE (  )
3. Peace in the world is certainly an *exigency* of the moment. TRUE (  ) FALSE (  )
4. The wolf is a *predatory* animal. TRUE (  ) FALSE (  )
5. An *aquiline* nose is straight. TRUE (  ) FALSE (  )
6. Vice is *anathema* to moral people. TRUE (  ) FALSE (  )

7.  It is easy to explain things to
    an *obtuse* person.                TRUE ( )   FALSE ( )
8.  Someone with *catholic* views is
    narrow-minded.                     TRUE ( )   FALSE ( )
9.  A large bank account *obviates*
    financial fears.                   TRUE ( )   FALSE ( )
10. *Erudite* people are well
    educated.                          TRUE ( )   FALSE ( )

**How Did You Do?** *Check Your Results.*

1—FALSE, 2—FALSE, 3—TRUE, 4—TRUE, 5—FALSE, 6—TRUE, 7—FALSE, 8—FALSE, 9—TRUE, 10—TRUE.

# *Third Day*

## TEST YOUR SPELLING

---

In a few moments you can find out whether your spelling is as good as it should be—or whether you make errors you're not even aware of!

---

### IS YOUR SPELLING
### AS GOOD AS YOU ARE?

**Test 8:** *These 10 Words Baffle Many People—Do You Know How to Spell Them?*

Which is correct:

1. (a) drunkeness,      *or* (b) drunkenness?
2. (a) embarassment,    *or* (b) embarrassment?
3. (a) all right,       *or* (b) alright?
4. (a) repetition,      *or* (b) repitition?
5. (a) occurrance,      *or* (b) occurrence?
6. (a) occassional,     *or* (b) occasional?
7. (a) separate,        *or* (b) seperate?
8. (a) cooly,           *or* (b) coolly?
9. (a) reccomend,       *or* (b) recommend?
10. (a) liquefy,         *or* (b) liquify?

**How Did You Do?** *Check Your Results.*

1—b. The adjective *drunken*, plus the ending *-ness*.
2—b. Note that both the *r* and *s* are doubled.
3—a. Only the two-word spelling is fully acceptable, no matter what the meaning.
4—a. Think of the verb form *repeat* to remember the correct vowel after the *p*.
5—b. Note the double *r* and *-ence* ending.
6—b. No reason for the double *s*, though most poor spellers are addicted to it.
7—a. Remember the crucial *a* by thinking of its synonym, *apart*.
8—b. *Cool* plus the adverbial ending *-ly*.
9—b. The verb *commend*, which everyone spells correctly, plus the prefix *re-*.
10—a. Only five verbs end in *-efy* rather than the common *-ify; liquefy, putrefy, rarefy, stupefy*, and, of course, *defy*.

**Test 9:** *Do You Recognize Incorrect Spelling?*

Find the *single* misspelled word in each line, cross it out, and rewrite it correctly.

1. superintendant, persistent, insistent, dependent, consistent. _____
2. supervise, advertise, despise, analize, memorize. _____
3. dissatisfied, dissimilar, dissapointed, disappear, misspelling, misspent. _____
4. niece, achieve, relieve, recieve, seize, leisure, weird. _____
5. indispensable, irritable, irresistable, dependable, inimitable. _____

**How Did You Do?** *Check Your Results.*

1. Change *superintendant* to *superintendent*.
These are the five *-ent* words that are most troublesome
to insecure spellers. The two most frequently misspelled
*-ance* words are *resistance* and *perseverance*.

2. Change *analize* to *analyze*.
The only two common words ending in *-yze* are *analyze*
and *paralyze*.

3. Change *dissapointed* to *disappointed*.
*Disappointed* and *disappear* are combinations of the prefix *dis-* and the roots *appoint* and *appear*—hence, no
reason for a double *s*. In the other words, however, the
double *s* is required because the roots start with *s*: *dis-*
plus *satisfied*, *dis-* plus *similar*, *mis-* plus *spelling*, *mis-* plus
*spent*.

4. Change *recieve* to *receive*.
The rule, you will recall, is "*i* before *e*, except after *c*."
Since there is an immediately preceding *c* in *receive*, *-ei*,
rather than *-ie*, is the correct pattern. True, there is no
*c* in *seize*, *leisure*, and *weird*, but these are the three
important exceptions to the rule.

5. Change *irresistable* to *irresistible*.
The *-able*, *-ible* problem is one of the thorniest in English spelling, and the five words offered here are the
ones that cause the most confusion.

# Fourth Day

## TEST YOUR GRAMMAR

---

Do you generally use words correctly? Are you usually *sure*—or only *half sure*? Let's put it to a test.

---

### DOES YOUR GRAMMAR
### MAKE A GOOD IMPRESSION?

No one's grammar is perfect, of course, but conspicuously poor English (such as some of the usages listed below) wrench the listener's attention away from *what* a speaker is saying and direct it to the *error* he is making.

**Test 10:** *Is Your English Free of Glaring Errors?*

Be honest with yourself. Do some of the following patterns occur with any frequency in your own speech? If you can check the NO box in most instances, consider yourself safe. On the other hand, wherever you must admit that you are addicted to a particular error, a little thought and concentration, plus an awareness of the principle involved, can quickly and permanently eliminate the incorrect pattern.

|  | DO YOU OFTEN |
|---|---|
| THE ERROR | SPEAK THIS WAY? |

1. He *done*, I *seen* . . .  YES ( ) NO ( )
2. *Irregardless* of what you say . . .  YES ( ) NO ( )
3. He *don't* like to . . .  YES ( ) NO ( )
4. *Him* and *me* can come . . .  YES ( ) NO ( )
5. When his mother and father *was* alive . . .  YES ( ) NO ( )
6. I *ain't* happy about it . . .  YES ( ) NO ( )
7. We *can't hardly* . . .  YES ( ) NO ( )
8. I don't need *no* money . . .  YES ( ) NO ( )
9. *This here* plan, *that there* statement . . .  YES ( ) NO ( )
10. *Them* books, *them* people . . .  YES ( ) NO ( )

**How Did You Do?** *Check Your Results.*

1. *Done* and *seen* may be used only after *has, have,* or *had,* i.e., in the *perfect tense.* The correct *past tense* of these verbs is *did* and *saw.*

2. The correct word is *regardless;* or, if you prefer to start with a negative prefix, say *irrespective.*

3. *Don't,* a contraction of *do not,* may be used only with a *plural* subject (or with the pronoun *I*). Say *doesn't* (a contraction of *does not*) with a *singular* subject: *he doesn't, she doesn't, it doesn't, the man doesn't,* etc.

4. *Him* and *me* are objective pronouns, as also are *her, us,* and *them,* and may not be used as *subjects* (i.e., before the verb). Say *He and I can come.*

5. Two words connected by *and* take a *plural* verb— his mother and father *were* alive, the book and pencil *are* hers, etc.

6. While *ain't* is a good serviceable word, it is never used by educated speakers except in jest.

7. *Hardly* and *scarcely* are negative words—when you use them, keep the verb affirmative. Say *can hardly, can scarcely,* etc.

8. Here again, the double negative must be avoided—say *I don't need any money*. How would you eliminate the error in these similar sentences? *I can't see no one; I won't go there no more; I didn't take none; I didn't talk to nobody; I didn't see it nowhere.*

9. Omit *here* and *there*—say *this plan, that statement.*

10. *Them* may not be used as an adjective—say *those* or *these.*

**Test 11:** *Are You Clear on Some of the Following Important Points of Correct English?*

The italicized word in some of the following sentences is used correctly—in others, it violates an established rule of grammar. Do you know which is which? If you can make at least six correct choices, your English is above average.

1. He's not as tall as *me*.    RIGHT ( )   WRONG ( )
2. You work faster than *her*. RIGHT ( )   WRONG ( )
3. Would you like to visit my brother and *I* tonight?    RIGHT ( )   WRONG ( )
4. If you don't feel well, why don't you *lay* down for a while?    RIGHT ( )   WRONG ( )
5. He felt so weak that he just *lay* asleep all day.    RIGHT ( )   WRONG ( )
6. Two new schools are now being built, but neither of them *is* finished.    RIGHT ( )   WRONG ( )
7. This is a *most* unique house.    RIGHT ( )   WRONG ( )
8. Let's keep this strictly between you and *me*.    RIGHT ( )   WRONG ( )

**How Did You Do?** *Check Your Results.*

1. WRONG. As you will see if you add the final implied word, "He's not as tall as *I* (am)."

2. WRONG. As before, if you finish the sentence you can determine the correct word—"You work faster than *she* (does)."

3. WRONG. You would say, ". . . visit *me*," not *I*; hence, ". . . visit my brother and *me*." When undecided about a pronoun following *and*, say it over, leaving out the preceding words, and you can't go wrong. For example: *He saw (John and) me* (not *I*); *We can do without (you and) her* (not *she*); *Can you talk to (them and) us* (not *we*)?

4. WRONG. *Lay* means *to place* (something), as *Lay the pillow on the bed*. When you mean *rest* or *recline*, say *lie*.

5. RIGHT. The past tense of *lie* (to recline or rest) is, strangely enough, *lay*, not *laid* or *lied*. The past of *lay* is *laid*: *They laid the foundation of the building this morning*.

6. RIGHT. *Neither of* means *neither one of*, so requires a singular verb. The same rule applies to *either of*.

7. WRONG. *Unique* means without a like or equal, so any modifying adjective is superfluous.

8. RIGHT. After *between*, which is a preposition, use only the *objective* forms of the pronoun—*me, him, her, us, them*. Other prepositions you must learn to be wary of, when a pronoun follows, are: *except, but* (meaning *except*), *to, with, without, for, from*, and *against*. Study these:

   a. No one's here *except us*.
   b. Everyone's satisifed *but her*.
   c. Will you speak *to* Sam and *me*?
   d. May I go *with* you and *him*?
   e. We can get along *without* you and *them*.

# *Fifth Day*

## JUST FOR FUN (I)

### *I. TEST YOUR FLUENCY*

How quickly can you call words to mind? Here is a reliable test of your vocabulary responsiveness. In five minutes or less, write next to each of the following words a word which starts with *R* and is essentially *opposite* in meaning to, or in contrast with, the given word. *Examples: walk-run; imaginary—real; square—round.*

1. slow _____
2. common _____
3. cooked _____
4. unprepared _____
5. front _____
6. forget _____
7. send _____
8. increase _____
9. left _____
10. green _____
11. polite _____
12. transient _____
13. wholesale _____
14. submit _____
15. dull _____
16. aggressive _____

17. careful     _____
18. work     _____
19. urban     _____
20. conform     _____

KEY: 1–rapid, 2–rare, 3–raw, 4–ready, 5–rear, 6–recollect, remember, *or* recall, 7–receive, retain, *or* rescind, 8–reduce *or* retard, 9–right, 10–ripe, 11–rude, 12–resident, 13–retail, 14–resist *or* rebel, 15–radiant, 16–recessive, reticent, retiring, *or* reluctant, 17–reckless, 18–rest, relax (ation), *or* recreation, 19–rural *or* rustic, 20–resist *or* rebel.

## II. THE NAME BEHIND THE WORD

*BOYCOTT:* Captain Charles C. Boycott had a run-in with some Irish farmers who refused to pay the exorbitant rents demanded by his company. The sons of Eire picketed Boycott's home and refused to let anyone work for him.

*GAT:* Richard Jordan Gatling invented the first machine gun in 1861.

*MARCEL WAVE:* Marcel was a famous French hairdresser who made a fortune out of his new idea in coiffures.

*SILHOUETTE:* Etienne de Silhouette was finance minister of France just before the Revolution. He insisted that the nobles lead *simpler* lives, thus saving money, which, of course, they could donate to the government. The *silhouette* (as it was later called) was invented at about this time and was obviously a very *simple* sort of portraiture. The connection of ideas appealed to the Parisian mind, and the minister's name was soon used to describe the new art form.

## III. DID YOU KNOW THAT—

*Italics* are so called because this kind of type was first used by the Italian, Aldus Manutius, famous printer of Venice.

*Drat it* is not so mild a curse as it may seem. It is a contraction of *May God rot it.*

Calling an attractive girl a *peach*, far from being modern slang, goes back at least to 1896.

In England a *streetcar* is called a *tram*; a *cookie jar* is known as a *biscuit barrel; molasses* is known as *treacle;* and the *movies* are called the *cinema.*

*Whiskey* is from the Irish *uisgebeatha* meaning *water of life.*

## IV. THINK OF WORDS

Can you think of 10 words ending in -ANK? Add *one or two letters only*, to fit each definition.

1. _____ank (free from writing; empty)
2. _____ank (disagreeably moist)
3. _____ank (slender)
4. _____ank (noise)
5. _____ank (trick)
6. _____ank (side of an animal)
7. _____ank (an arm for winding)
8. _____ank (lower part of the leg)
9. _____ank (candid)
10. _____ank (board)

Now your problem is to think of a word *opposed* in meaning to the definition offered. The initial letter is supplied.

11. a_____ (passive)
12. b_____ (dull)

13. c_____ (throw)
14. d_____ (stay)
15. e_____ (leave)
16. f_____ (smile)
17. g_____ (sad)
18. h_____ (proud)
19. i_____ (community)
20. j_____ (senile)
21. k_____ (be ignorant)
22. l_____ (stiff)
23. m_____ (phobia)
24. n_____ (sophisticated)
25. o_____ (closed)
26. p_____ (meek)
27. q_____ (ordinary)
28. r_____ (common)
29. s_____ (complex)
30. t_____ (wild)
31. u_____ (unique)
32. v_____ (valuable)
33. w_____ (ruddy)
34. y_____ (white of an egg)
35. z_____ (lowest point)

KEY:  1–blank, 2–dank, 3–lank, 4–clank, 5–prank, 6–flank, 7–crank, 8–shank, 9–frank, 10–plank, 11–active, alive, *or* alert, 12–bright, 13–catch, 14–depart, 15–enter, 16–frown, 17–gay *or* glad, 18–humble, 19–individual, 20–juvenile, 21–know, 22–lithe *or* lax, 23–mania, 24–naïve, 25–open (ed), 26–proud, 27–quaint *or* queer, 28–rare, 29–simple, 30–tame, 31–universal, 32–valueless, 33–wan *or* white, 34–yolk *or* yellow, 35–zenith.

# PART II

# *Say It Right!*

From your pronunciation of certain common and frequently used English words, people often form their first impressions of your educational background, of your ability and intelligence, perhaps even of your personality. This is unfortunate and in many instances probably illogical; what a person says is certainly a much more reasonable criterion of his worth than how he says it. But human nature is not always reasonable, and listeners tend to jump to sweeping conclusions from quick impressions of the way you speak.

*Your pronunciation, for this reason, always either adds to or detracts from the power and persuasiveness of your ideas.*

Consider the importance of pronunciation from another point of view. The effectiveness of a spoken thought stems not only from the thought itself or from the words in which it is presented, but also—often even more so—from the self-assurance of the person who is speaking. *Confidence and security about the correctness of your pronunciation can be a vital factor in helping you put across your ideas successfully.*

So the chapters in Part II have a number of aims:

▶To give you practical training in the correct pronunciation of some of the most troublesome words in the English language.

▶To offer you practice in these words, so that correct pronunciation becomes habitual and completely natural.

▶To root out of your speech—permanently and completely—every possibility of unconscious error.

▶To settle any doubts or confusion you may have about certain pronunciation demons.

▶And thus, in total, to increase your self-assurance whenever you give voice to your ideas.

# *Sixth Day*

## CAN YOU PASS THIS EASY PRONUNCIATION TEST?

Your reaction to nine significant English words will tell you a great deal about your pronunciation habits.

### *TEST YOUR PRONUNCIATION*

High on the list of troublesome words are nine demons that have a diabolical ability to trap the unwary speaker. How do you pronounce each one? Make your decision not on the basis of what you may think is correct but solely in accordance with what you would say in ordinary conversation.

[The symbol ə indicates the very slight vowel heard in the first syllable of *commit* (kə-MIT′) or the last syllable of *Linda* (LIN′-də)].

1. radiator
   (a) RAD′-ee-ay-tər
   (b) RAY′-dee-ay-tər
2. mischievous
   (a) miss-CHEE′-vee-əs
   (b) MISS′-chə-vəs
3. genuine
   (a) JEN′-yoo-in
   (b) JEN′-yoo-wine
4. comparable
   (a) KOM′-pə-rə-bəl
   (b) kəm-PAR′-ə-bəl
   (ĂR as in *carriage*)

5. chiropodist
    (a) kə-ROP'-ə-dist
    (b) tchə-ROP'-ə-dist
6. human
    (a) YOO'-mən
    (b) HYOO'-mən
7. impotent
    (a) im-PO'-tənt
    (b) IM'-pə-tənt

8. accessory
    (a) a-SESS'-ər-ee
    (b) ak-SESS'-ər-ee
9. orgy
    (a) OR'-jee
    (b) OR'-gee (*g* as in *game*)

KEY: 1–b, 2–b, 3–a, 4–a, 5–a, 6–b, 7–b, 8–b, 9–a.


## SAY IT ALOUD

Knowing the correct forms is only half the battle in your conquest of pronunciation demons. The other, and possibly more important, half is developing the habit of *using* the correct forms without hesitation whenever you speak. An awareness that the first *A* of *radiator* is pronounced as it is in *bay*, or that *mischievous* has three syllables rather than four, is of little benefit if you still unthinkingly say RAD'-ee-ay-tər and miss-CHEE'-vee-əs in your everyday conversation. Only practice will permanently root these mispronunciations out of your speech. *So say these words several times aloud*, hear them correctly in your own voice, push them deep into your consciousness.

1. radiator—RAY'-dee-ay-tər
2. mischievous—MISS'-chə-vəs
3. genuine—JEN'-yoo-in
4. comparable—KOM'-pə-rə-bəl
5. chiropodist—kə-ROP'-ə-dist
6. human-HYOO'-mən
7. impotent—IM'-pə-tənt
8. accessory—ak-SESS'-ər-ee
9. orgy-OR'-jee

So far you have been practicing the correct sounds of these tricky demons with a proper wariness and a certain self-consciousness. Suppose you were uttering the words casually in conversation; would you unhesitatingly avoid the pitfalls? Let us see. Read these phrases aloud, quickly and naturally—and, of course, correctly.

> a hot radiator
> human mischievousness
> genuine impotence
> incomparably skillful chiropodist
> wild orgies
> optional accessories

## WATCH YOUR ACCENT

Each of the nine words covered up to this point serves as a warning sign of a kind of error effective speakers have learned to avoid.

*Comparable*, for example, is one of a group of demons ending in *-able* that cause the most plaguing type of accent trouble. Your final and complete conquest of this group will require patience and tenacity. Accenting the indicated syllable may at first seem almost superhumanly difficult; but it will become gradually easier with practice. Listen to yourself carefully, or ask a friend to listen to you, as you say the following words aloud; make sure you are accenting the capitalized syllable and not the one after it.

1. COM'-parable
2. PREF'-erable
3. AM'-icable
4. HOS'-pitable
5. AD'-mirable
6. LAM'-entable
7. EX'-plicable
8. AP'-plicable
9. FOR'-midable
10. REP'-utable
11. DES'-picable

In other forms of these words, the accent remains on the same syllable: *in*-COM'-*parable*, *in*-HOS'-*pitable*, *dis*-REP'-*utable*, COM'-*parability*, etc.

The one exception to the group, *disputable*, may be pronounced with the accent either on the first or on the second syllable: DIS'-*putable* or *dis*-PU'-*table*. So also the negative form: *in*-DIS'-*putable* or *indis*-PU'-*table*.

When you are sure you have all these words under effortless control, try reading these phrases aloud. Can you, without any great difficulty, keep the accent where it belongs?

> admirable results
> amicable settlement
> lamentable error
> despicable dishonesty
> applicable examples

# *Seventh Day*

## MORE PRACTICE IN GOOD PRONUNCIATION

---

Here are 25 important words that poor speakers say in a slovenly fashion. How about you?

---

### *SAY IT CLEARLY*

Now let us look at another group of pronunciation demons: words, like *accessory*, that may tempt unwary speakers into omitting essential letters. This leads to the kind of slovenly articulation that robs speech of forcefulness. Say each word aloud with particular attention to the italicized letter, *which should be sounded distinctly.*

|  |  |  |
|---|---|---|
| 1. | a*C*cessory | ak-SESS′-ər-ee |
| 2. | su*C*cin*C*t | sək-SINGKT′ |
| 3. | a*C*cept | ak-SEPT′ |
| 4. | a*C*cede | ak-SEED′ |
| 5. | a*C*celerator | ak-SEL′-ə-ray-tər |
| 6. | lib*R*ary | LYE′-brer-ee |
| 7. | Feb*R*uary | FEB′-roo-er-ee |
| 8. | len*G*th | LENGKTH |
| 9. | stren*G*th | STRENGKTH |
| 10. | wi*D*th | WIDTH |

| 11. | goverNment | GUV'-ərn-mənt |
| 12. | gEography | jee-OG'-rə-fee |
| 13. | Eleven | ə-LEV'-ən |
| 14. | asKed | ASKT |
| 15. | piCture | PIK'-chər |
| 16. | probaBly | PROB'-əb-lee |
| 17. | ruIn (2 syllables) | ROO'-ən |
| 18. | poEm (2 syllables) | PO'-əm |
| 19. | recoGnize | REK'-əg-nize |
| 20. | particUlar | pər-TIK'-yə-lər |
| 21. | figUre | FIG'-yər |
| 22. | regUlar | REG'-yə-lər |
| 23. | accUrate | AK'-yə-rət |
| 24. | manUfacture | man-yə-FAK'-chər |
| 25. | kepT | KEPT |

In this type of word especially, only constant repetition of the correct form is likely to be effective in changing habits. So be relentless in your practice; read the entire list *aloud* as often as you think necessary to engrave the crucial letter of each word on your mind. Then check on the success of your practice by reading the following phrases quickly. Are you saying all the sounds that should be heard?

> succinct and acceptable analysis
> length and width of the library
> February the eleventh
> recognized the government
> kept the picture
> accurate figures
> regular manufactures
> of particular strength
> probably ruined the poem
> asked for geography

Let us now cruise along over the remaining categories,

with the understanding that final and complete mastery can be achieved only from repeated practice. Single out for special attention those groups in which you feel weakest, and be generous with your time and effort. Frequent repetition of the words *aloud* will make correct habits so deep-seated that the possibility of error, even in the heat of animated conversation, will be reduced to the vanishing point.

## DON'T SAY TOO MUCH

In the previous section, your practice was devoted to words in which speakers often casually ignore essential letters that should be clearly pronounced. This section, on the contrary, offers the kind of demon—*mischievous* is a typical example—in which some people tend to insert sounds that aren't there.

Read each word in Column I aloud. Check your pronunciation by referring to the correct form in Column II. Are you saying no more than necessary? Make sure that you avoid the incorrect form listed in Column III.

| I | II. Say: | III. Do Not Say: |
|---|---|---|
| 1. mischievous | MISS'-chə-vəs | miss-CHEE'-vee-əs |
| 2. grievous | GREE'-vəs | GREE'-vee-əs |
| 3. film | FILM (1 syllable) | FILL'-əm |
| 4. elm | ELM (1 syllable) | ELL'-əm |
| 5. drowned | DROWND (1 syllable) | DROWN'-dəd |
| 6. percolator | PUR'-kə-lay-tər | PUR'-kyə-lay-tər |
| 7. attacked | ə-TAKT' | ə-TAK'-təd |
| 8. athletic | ath-LET'-ic | ath-ə-LET'-ic |
| 9. athlete | ATH'-leet | ATH'-ə-leet |
| 10. just | JUST | JIST |

| 11. get     | GET      | GIT       |
| 12. wrestle | RESS'-əl | RASS'-əl  |

## SOUND YOUR H

In a few English words, such as *honor* and *honest*, the letter *H* is, of course, silent; but in the following words the *H* should be clearly pronounced. Try these aloud.

| | |
|---|---|
| 1. *h*uman | 6. *h*umid |
| 2. *h*umanity | 7. *h*umidity |
| 3. *h*umane | 8. *h*uge |
| 4. *h*umor | 9. *h*umble |
| 5. *h*umorous | 10. *h*omage |

In *herb*, the *H* is usually silent, but it is equally correct to sound it; say either *'erb* or *herb*.

## BEWARE OF G

*G* is a tricky confusing letter. Often it is hard, as in *game*. Just as often, especially before vowels, *E*, *I*, and *Y*, it is soft, as in *gem*, *gin*, and *gymnasium*.

Beware particularly of the following words, in each of which *G* is soft, with the sound of *J*.

| | |
|---|---|
| 1. orgy | 5. intelligentsia |
| 2. gesture | 6. gibberish |
| 3. gesticulate | 7. gibe |
| 4. turgid | 8. longevity (lon-JEV'-ə-tee) |

And beware, too, of these, in which *G* has the same sound as the *S* in *pleasure, treasure*, or *measure*, indicated usually by the symbol *ZH*. Say *pleasure* several times aloud, noting the characteristic sound of the *S*; then give the same sound to *G* in each of the following.

1. garage          gə-RAHZH′
2. barrage         bə-RAHZH′
3. camouflage      KAM′-ə-flahzh
4. massage         mə-SAHZH′
5. corsage         kor-SAHZH′
6. sabotage        SAB′-ə-tahzh
7. prestige        press-TEEZH′
8. cortege         kor-TEZH′

Practice aloud with an alert ear to make sure you are *not* pronouncing the G like a *J*; the tongue should hang slack in the mouth rather than hitting the front of the palate, and the result should be fairly liquid.

## KEEP SOUNDS UNTWISTED

In eight special words, poor speakers tend to transpose sounds, pronouncing them in incorrect order, often with humorous results. Try these, noting the instructions.

1. *bronchial*—BRONG′-kee-el, *not* BRON′-ə-kəl (Note that *ch-* precedes the *-i.*)

2. *superfluous*—soo-PUR′-floo-əs, *not* soo-PUR′-fə-ləs (Note that *l-* precedes the *-u.*)

3. *larynx*—LĂR′-inx (ă as in *hat*), *not* LAHR′-nix (Note that *y-* precedes the *-n.*)

4. *irrelevant*—ir-REL′-ə-vənt, *not* ir-REV′-ə-lənt (Note that *l-* precedes the *-v.*)

5. *modern*—MOD′-ərn, *not* MOD′-rən (note again that *e-* precedes the *-r.*)

6. *pattern*—PAT′-ərn, *not* PAT′-rən (Note again that *e-* precedes the *-r.*)

7. *perspiration*—pur-spə-RAY′-shən, *not* press-pə-RAY′-shən (Note that *e-* precedes the *-r.*)

8. *prescription*—prə-SKRIP′-shən, *not* pər-SKRIP′-shən (Note that in this word, on the other hand, *r-* precedes the *-e.*)

## GET STRAIGHT ON -ILE

Most words that end in *-ile* are preferably pronounced with the ending *-ill*, to rhyme with *mill*, with the exceptions noted later. Practice the following by saying them aloud over and over again.

| | | |
|---|---|---|
| 1. | fragile | FRAJ'-ill |
| 2. | servile | SUR'-vill |
| 3. | versatile | VUR'-sə-till |
| 4. | fertile | FUR'-till |
| 5. | imbecile | IM'-bə-sill |
| 6. | hostile | HOS'-till |
| 7. | sterile | STER'-ill |
| 8. | docile | DOSS'-ill |
| 9. | agile | AJ'-ill |
| 10. | futile | FYOO'-till |
| 11. | virile | VIR'-ill, *not* VER'-ill |

In the following exceptions, the last syllable rhymes with *mile*.

| | | |
|---|---|---|
| 1. | infantile | IN'-fən-tile |
| 2. | senile | SEE'-nile |
| 3. | profile | PRO'-file |
| 4. | exile | EK'-sile *or* EG'-zile |
| 5. | reconcile | REK'-ən-sile |
| 6. | crocodile | KROK'-ə-dile |
| 7. | turnstile | TURN'-stile |
| 8. | bibliophile | BIB'-lee-ə-file |

In four special words, you may rhyme the ending either with *mill* or with *mile*. Use whichever form sounds better to you.

| | | |
|---|---|---|
| 1. | juvenile | 3. mercantile |
| 2. | textile | 4. domicile |

# *Eighth Day*

## STILL MORE WORDS THAT FOOL THE UNWARY

You complete your understanding in the principles of correct pronunciation by examining four final categories of English words; then you check the success of your learning in Part II by taking a pronunciation test that most unsophisticated speakers would do very poorly on.

---

### *DON'T MISPLACE ACCENTS*

The position of the accent in English words is more often a stumbling block and a source of doubt and confusion than any other single factor. Here are 20 words that cause a lot of trouble.

1. impotent       IM'-pə-tənt
2. impious        IM'-pee-əs
3. infamous       IN'-fə-məs
4. influence      IN'-floo-ənce
5. distribute     dis-TRIB'-yət
6. affluence      AF'-floo-ənce
7. awry           ə-RYE'
8. remonstrate    rə-MON'-strate

| | | |
|---|---|---|
| 9. | deficit | DEF'-ə-sit |
| 10. | champion | CHAM'-pee-ən |
| 11. | integral | IN'-tə-grəl |
| 12. | municipal | myoo-NISS'-ə-pəl |
| 13. | intricate | IN'-trə-kit |
| 14. | intricacy | IN'-trə-kə-see |
| 15. | caricature | KĂR'-ə-kə-choor (ĂR as in *carriage*) |
| 16. | robust | rə-BUST' |
| 17. | acumen | ə-KYOO'-mən |
| 18. | plebeian | plə-BEE'-ən |
| 19. | ignominious | ig-nə-MIN'-ee-əs |
| 20. | dirigible | DIR'-ə-jə-bəl |

In the following eight words you have greater freedom in placing the accent.

| | | |
|---|---|---|
| 1. | exquisite | EX'-kwi-zit *or* ex-KWIZ'-it |
| 2. | adult | ə-DULT' *or* AD'-ult |
| 3. | inquiry | in-KWY'-ree *or* IN'-kwə-ree |
| 4. | aspirant | as-PIRE'-ənt *or* ASS'-pə-rənt |
| 5. | incognito | in-KOG'-nə-tō *or* in-kəg-NEE'-tō (ō as in *go*) |
| 6. | secretive | sə-KREE'-tiv *or* SEEK'-rə-tiv |
| 7. | acclimate | ə-KLY'-mət *or* AK'-lə-mayt |
| 8. | address (as in *name and address*) | ə-DRESS' *or* AD'-ress; as a verb, or with other meanings: ə-DRESS' *only* |

## DON'T BE MISLED BY CH

*Chiropodist*, you have learned, starts with the sound of *K* despite the spelling *CH*. In the following words the deceptive *CH* is always pronounced as a *K*.

| | | |
|---|---|---|
| 1. | chasm | KAZ'-əm |
| 2. | machinations | mak-ə-NAY'-shənz |

3. chaos        KAY'-oss
4. archipelago    ahr-kə-PEL'-ə-go

### GET STRAIGHT ON A'S

In *radiator*, as you now know, the first syllable rhymes with *bay:* RAY'-dee-ay-tər. The same is true of *aviator* (AY'-vee-ay-tər) and *verbatim* (vər-BAY'-təm). But in the following nine words you may use either the *A* of *bay* or the *A* of *hat*.

1. data          DAY'-tə *or* DAT'-ə
2. status       STAY'-təs *or* STAT'-əs
3. fracas       FRAY'-kəs *or* FRAK'-əs
4. ignoramus   ig-nə-RAY'-məs *or* ig-nə-RAM'-əs
5. ultimatum   ul-tə-MAY'-təm *or* ul-tə-MAT'-əm
6. strata       STRAY'-tə *or* STRAT'-ə
7. pro rata     pro RAY'-tə *or* pro RAT'-ə
8. gratis        GRAY'-təs *or* GRAT'-əs
9. apparatus   ap-ə-RAY'-təs *or* ap-ə-RAT'-əs

### SPEAK UNAFFECTEDLY

Here is a final group of seven words in which the choice of pronunciation is a source of uncertainty to many people. The forms listed in Column I are recommended because they are popular, inconspicuous, unaffected—and therefore safe. On the other hand, the Column II pronunciations are prevalent in some sections of the country and especially on certain social levels; use them if your instinctive preference inclines you strongly in that direction and if you are quite sure your pronunciation will not set you apart from those with whom you usually talk.

| | I. *Recommended:* | II. *Also Correct, but Conspicuous:* |
|---|---|---|
| 1. either | EE'-thər | EYE'-thər |

| | | |
|---|---|---|
| 2. neither | NEE′-thər | NYE′-thər |
| 3. aunt | ANT | AHNT |
| 4. vase | VAYZ *or* VAYS | VAHZ |
| 5. tomato | tə-MAY′-tō | tə-MAH′-tō |
| | | (ō as in *go*) |
| 6. rather | RA′-thər | RAH′-thər |
| | (rhymes with *gather*) | (rhymes with *father*) |
| 7. chauffeur | SHO′-fər | shə-FUR′ |

## TEST YOUR LEARNING

We have thoroughly explored twelve categories of demons that are the most devilish and the most troublesome in the entire English language. These words, more than any others, create doubt and confusion.

If you have worked hard on Part II, if you have begun to form new habits through repeated practice, then these words are no longer demons for you. They are no longer a source of possible error, no longer a cause of anxiety or lack of self-confidence.

Let us put the results of your study to a test. Here is a representative sampling of the words covered in Part II. Are you able now, unhestitatingly and unerringly, to make a correct choice?

1. genuine
   (a) JEN′-yoo-wine
   (b) JEN′-yoo-in
2. manufacture
   (a) man-ə-FAK′-chər
   (b) man-yə-FAK′-chər
3. preferable
   (a) PREF′-ər-ə-bəl
   (b) prə-FER′-ə-bəl
4. figure
   (a) FIG′-ər
   (b) FIG′-yər
5. grievous
   (a) GREE′-vəs
   (b) GREE′-vee-əs
6. athletic
   (a) ath-ə-LET′-ic
   (b) ath-LET′-ic
7. huge
   (a) HYOOJ
   (b) YOOJ
8. gesture
   (a) GES′-chər
   (b) JES′-chər

9. prestige
   (a) press-TEEZH'
   (b) press-TEEDJ'
10. bronchial
    (a) BRON'-ə-kəl
    (b) BRONG'-kee-əl
11. fertile
    (a) FUR'-till
    (b) FUR'-tile
12. senile
    (a) SEN'-ill
    (b) SEE'-nile
13. impious
    (a) IM'-pee-əs
    (b) im-PY'-əs
14. awry
    (a) ə-RYE'
    (b) AW'-ree
15. intricacy
    (a) in-TRIK'-ə-see
    (b) IN'-trə-kə-see
16. dirigible
    (a) DIR'-ə-jə-bəl
    (b) de-RIJ'-e-bəl
17. machinations
    (a) mak-ə-NAY'-shənz
    (b) match-ə-NAY'-shənz
18. aviator
    (a) AV'-ee-ay-tər
    (b) AY'-vee-ay-tər

KEY: 1–b, 2–b, 3–a, 4–b, 5–a, 6–b, 7–a, 8–b, 9–a, 10–b, 11–a, 12–b, 13–a, 14–a, 15–b, 16– a, 17–a, 18–b.

# NINTH DAY

## JUST FOR FUN (II)

### I. IT'S MURDER!

Killing anyone is generally illegal, usually unethical, and almost always unpleasant. But murder goes back at least as far as Cain and Abel and even in the most civilized of countries is always part of the current scene.

Here are 10 of the most popular victims of murder in one column, and the words that identify the type of killing in another column. How successfully can you match the word with the deed?

1. whole groups of races of people    (a) sororicide
2. one's mother    (b) uxoricide
3. one's father    (c) vermicide
4. one's brother    (d) homicide
5. one's sister    (e) parricide
6. either parent or anyone in a    (f) fratricide
parental capacity
7. one's king    (g) genocide
8. any human being    (h) patricide
9. one's wife    (i) regicide
10. worms, especially the intestinal,    (j) matricide
parasitic variety

KEY:   1–g, 2–j, 3–h, 4–f, 5–a, 6–e, 7–i, 8–d, 9–b, 10–c.

## II. ILLOGICAL EXPRESSIONS

COMMENCEMENT comes at the END of a college course.
We SAIL to Europe by STEAMship.
Some airplanes can LAND on WATER.
A hospital is MANNED by WOMEN.
What was in yesterday's paper is OLD NEWS.
Something GROWS SMALLER.

## III. THE 13 WORDS MOST OFTEN MISPRONOUNCED

There are many hundreds of thousands of words in our language—and though few of us know or use all of them, it is likely that thousands of different ones pass our lips in a week's conversation.

Here's what is startling—out of these thousands of words in daily use, *exactly 13* are more frequently mispronounced by the average speaker than any other words, common or uncommon, in the entire English language.

This statistic has been discovered through investigations made in vocabulary-improvement classes in the Division of General Education of New York University; and term after term, with different students, the result is confirmed—it's always the same thirteen words that cause the most trouble.

You will find this most-sinned-against baker's dozen of English words on the next page—and a chance to find out whether you tend to make the same mistakes as most other people. Check the pronunciation you honestly and habitually use, then compare your results with the key below. If you're average, you should get no more than 4 or 5 right; 6 to 8 correct choices will indicate a high degree of linguistic sophistication; 9 to 12 will mean that your command of English is remarkable; and a perfect score will mark you as unique, no less.

1. orgy (drunken revelry): (a) OR'-jee, *or* (b) OR'-gee?

2. human: (a) YOO'-mən, *or* (b) HYOO'-mən?

3. forte (strong point): (a) FOR'-tay, *or* (b) FORT?

4. genuine: (a) JEN'-yoo-win, *or* (b) JEN'-yoo-wine?

5. acumen (mental keenness): (a) ə-KYOO'-mən, *or* (b) AK'-yoo-mən?

6. admirable: (a) ad-MIRE'-ə-bəl, *or* (b) AD'-mə-rə-bəl?

7. mischievous: (a) mis-CHEE'-vee-əs, *or* (b) MIS'-chə-vəs?

8. radiator: (a) RAY'-dee-ay-tər, *or* (b) RAD'-ee-ay-tər?

9. grimace (facial contortion): (a) grə-MAYCE', *or* (b) GRIM'-əss?

10. impious (against religion): (a) im-PYE'-əs, *or* (b) IM'-pee-əs?

11. finis (the end): (a) fee-NEE', (b) FIN'-iss, *or* (c) FYE'-niss?

12. naïveté (artlessness): (a) NAY'-və-tee, (b) nah-eev-TAY', *or* (c) nay-VET'?

13. integral (essential): (a) IN'-tə-grəl, (b) in-TEG'-rəl , *or* (c) in-TEE'-grəl?

KEY:  1—a, 2—b, 3—b, 4—a, 5—a, 6—b, 7—b, 8—a, 9—a, 10—b, 11—c, 12—b, 13—a.

## IV. WHAT KIND OF SPELLER ARE YOU?

English spelling is no cinch, and the 10 demons that follow may throw you if you don't keep an eye peeled.

Check the pattern you trust, then see below for answers.

1. (a) embarrassing, (b) embarassing, (c) embarrasing
2. (a) superintendent, (b) superintendant
3. (a) catagory, (b) category
4. (a) supercede, (b) superceed, (c) supersede
5. (a) annoint, (b) anoint
6. (a) absence, (b) abscence
7. (a) occurrance, (b) occurrence, (c) occurence
8. (a) exhillarate, (b) exhilirate, (c) exhilarate
9. (a) dispair, (b) despair
10. (a) dissipate, (b) dissapate, (c) disippate

KEY: 1–a, 2–a, 3–b, 4–c, 5–b, 6–a, 7–b, 8–c, 9–b, 10–a.
(See Part IV to learn special tricks for improving your spelling.)

# PART III

# *Improve Your Vocabulary!*

Vocabulary is important! Success not only in school and college, but also in one's professional and business life, has an eminently logical connection with the number of words one knows and can recognize and use.

So in Part III we get down to some intensive work in vocabulary-building.

# *Tenth Day*

## A SIMPLE PROGRAM FOR VOCABULARY IMPROVEMENT

---

To increase your vocabulary at a prodigious rate, you must learn to be on the alert for new words.

---

### *VOCABULARY IS IMPORTANT!*

In our modern world, the person with a good vocabulary has a better chance of success, other things being equal—a better chance of success not only in his school career but also when he gets out into the business or professional world.

Let us take a look at some of the evidence that points to this intimate relationship between vocabulary and scholastic, business, and professional success.

Research has established that the person who scores high in vocabulary is likely to possess above-average mental endowment. A vocabulary test provides as reliable a measure of intelligence as any combination of the three units in the Stanford-Binet I.Q. tests, according to Professor Lewis S. Terman, one of the foremost authorities in the field.

At the University of Illinois, entering students are routinely given a short vocabulary test. From the results, an accurate prediction can be made of probable academic successs—or lack of success—over the entire four-year college course.

At many other universities, groups of freshmen are put into experimental classes for the sole purpose of increasing their knowledge of English words. These students do far better in their sophomore, junior, and senior years than groups who have not received vocabulary training.

The Human Engineering Laboratory, an institution devoted to the investigation of people's aptitudes, tested the vocabularies of 100 young men in the graduating class of the Business School of a large university. Five years later, a survey of the careers of these 100 students revealed this spectacular pair of statistics: (1) every senior who had scored in the upper 10 percent of the group had become an executive; (2) not a single young man whose score was in the lowest 25 percent had attained an executive position.

The Laboratory, after testing the vocabularies of thousands of people in all age groups and in all walks of life, found that *the only common characteristic of successful people in this country was an unusual grasp of the meanings of words;* that the men and women drawing the highest salaries consistently made the highest scores. Consider very thoughtfully the explanation offered by Dr. Johnson O'Connor, director of the Laboratory:

"Why do large vocabularies characterize executives and possibly outstanding men and women in other fields? The final answer seems to be that words are the instruments by means of which men and women grasp the thoughts of others and with which they do much of their own thinking. They are the tools of thought."

The pages that follow will blueprint for you the most effective and productive techniques for permanently increasing *your* stock of the instruments of thinking and for sharpening your ability to grasp the thoughts of others. They will show you how to become more persuasive.

Systematically increasing your vocabulary, you will discover, can bring you unexpected dividends of personal satisfaction and self-fulfillment; it can be pleasurable and exciting perhaps beyond your fondest hopes.

## TAKE THIS VOCABULARY TEST

You are probably curious to learn how your own vocabulary stacks up against that of other people.

To find out, take this simple 10-minute test.

Below you will see 25 phrases, each containing an italicized word. Check what you consider the correct definition of every word with which you have any familiarity, however slight; omit an answer, however, if the italicized word is totally unfamiliar.

1. *disheveled* appearance: (a) untidy, (b) fierce, (c) foolish, (d) unhappy

2. a *baffling* problem: (a) difficult, (b) simple, (c) puzzling, (d) old, (e) new

3. extremely *lenient* parents: (a) tall, (b) not strict, (c) wise, (d) neglectful, (e) severe

4. an *audacious* attempt: (a) useless, (b) bold, (c) unwise, (d) crazy, (e) necessary

5. *agile* climber: (a) lively, (b) tired, (c) skillful, (d) careful, (e ) fast

6. *prevalent* disease: (a) dangerous, (b) catching, (c) childhood, (d) fatal, (e) widespread

7. *ominous* report: (a) loud, (b) threatening, (c) untrue, (d) serious, (e) unpleasant

8. an *incredible* story: (a) true), (b) interesting, (c) well-known, (d) unbelievable, (e) unknown

9. will *supersede* the old law: (a) enforce, (b) specify penalties for, (c) take the place of, (d) repeal, (e) continue in force

10. an *anonymous* donor: (a) generous, (b) stingy, (c) considerate, (d) one whose name is not known, (e) reluctant

11. an *indefatigable* worker: (a) well-paid, (b) conscientious, (c) courteous, (d) tireless, (e) pleasant

12. a *loquacious* woman: (a) motherly, (b) attractive, (c) homely, (d) seductive, (e) talkative

13. living in *affluence:* (a) filth, (b) countrified surroundings, (c) fear, (d) wealth, (e) poverty

14. to *simulate* interest: (a) pretend, (b) feel, (c) lose, (d) stir up, (e) ask for

15. a *congenital* deformity: (a) disfiguring (b) crippling, (c) slight, (d) incurable, (e) occurring at or during birth

16. took an *unequivocal* stand: (a) indecisive, (b) unexplainable, (c) unexpected, (d) definite, (e) hard to understand

17. *vicarious* enjoyment: (a) complete, (b) unspoiled, (c) occurring from a feeling of identification with another, (d) long-continuing, (e) temporary

18. *anachronous* garb: (a) absurd, (b) religious, (c) belonging to a different time, (d) out of place, (e) unusual

19. his *iconoclastic* phase: (a) artistic, (b) sneering at tradition, (c) troubled, (d) juvenile, (e) emotional

20. *semantic* confusion: (a) relating to the meanings of words, (b) relating to hearing, (c) relating to emotions, (d) relating to mathematics, (e) relating to vision

21. *cavalier* treatment: (a) polite, (b) high-handed, (c) negligent, (d) incomplete, (e) expensive

22. an *anomalous* situation: (a) dangerous, (b) intriguing, (c) uncommon, (d) pleasant, (e) tragic

23. his *laconic* reply: (a) immediate, (b) truthful, (c) terse and meaningful, (d) unintelligible (e) angry

24. an unusually *gregarious* person: (a) calm, (b) company-loving, (c) untrustworthy, (d) vicious, (e) self-sacrificing

25. the *cacophony* of the city: (a) political administration, (b) crowded living conditions, (c) cultural advantages, (d) harsh sounds, (e) foul odors

KEY: 1–a, 2–c, 3–b, 4–b, 5–a, 6–e, 7–b, 8–d, 9–c, 10–d, 11–d, 12–e, 13–d, 14–a, 15–e, 16– d, 17–c, 18–c, 19–b, 20–a, 21–b, 22–c, 23–c, 24–b, 25–d.

SCORING:  0–6 correct answers—*Below Average*
7–13 correct answers—*Average*
14–20 correct answers—*Above Average*
21–25 correct answers—*Superior*

## *HOW TO MAKE NEW WORDS COME ALIVE*

Learning new words is a lot easier than you may think—provided you go about it in the right way.

The secret of successful vocabulary building is *repetition.*

To add a new word to your vocabulary so that it really sticks there—permanently, unforgettably, usefully—you must see or hear that word in many different contexts and in variety of different forms.

Your first contact with a new word will be a fuzzy one—you will see in it no more than a meaningless pattern of syllables, a lifeless collection of letters. But at each successive contact, if the word is an integral part of a sentence, an idea, a thought, you will feel more and more life in the once-dead syllables, until finally you will be able to make an instantaneous mental reaction every time you read the word on a page of print or hear it from somebody's lips.

You will then have taken the first crucial step toward getting on friendly terms with a new word; you will have made it part of your *recognition vocabulary.*

Your attitude toward the word has thus far been a passive one. But you must also develop an active attitude. You must begin to use the word. You must learn to call it forth from the recesses of your recognition vocabulary whenever, in thinking, speaking, or writing, you have a use for it. You must, in short, add it to your *functional vocabulary.*

Here are the steps that will help you do all these things.

**Step 1:** *Consider Each New Word a Challenge*

There is always a great temptation to ignore an unfamiliar word that you meet in your reading—to skip over it quickly and blindly if you can manage to extract some meaning, however slight, from the sentence or paragraph in which it occurs. *Resist this temptation.* Consider a new word a red light, a stop sign, a challenge to your imagination and ingenuity. Look at it, become familiar with its appearance, puzzle out its possible meaning from the context.

Try this now. Here are eight words that may be new to you. They are admittedly not everyday terms, and they are fairly complex in meaning; indeed, they have been chosen for these very qualities. Examine the sentence fragment in which each word appears, arrive at a probable or possible meaning, even make a wild guess if you wish—but at least come to grips with the challenge with which each of the words will confront you.

1. felt so listless, so completely *enervated:* (a) weakened, (b) tired, (c) confused, (d) defeated

2. such contemptible *sycophancy:* (a) insincere virtuousness, (b) self-seeking flattery, (c) pretense at genuineness, (d) sneakiness and spying

3. no organic disease, but a kind of persistent *hypochondria:* (a) illness of psychological origin, (b) morbid fancies that one is ill, though physically healthy, (c) attitude of unhealthy fear, (d) state of mental delusions

4. so withdrawn and *introverted* as to seem positively unsociable: (a) preferring solitude to the company of others, (b) insulting and hostile in conversation, (c) morbidly silent, (d) more interested in one's thoughts, feelings, etc., than in the outside world

5. such outspoken *misogyny* as to alienate, if not repel, all women: (a) fear of women, (b) hatred of women, (c) pursuit of women, (d) discourtesy to women

6. her *altruistic* generosity: (a) showing more concern for the welfare of others than for one's own welfare, (b) unlimited, (c) pretended and insincere, (d) well advertised

7. his name, which is *anathema* to all patriots: (a) an object of speculation, (b) an object of the deepest loathing, (c) an object of respect and devotion, (d) an example of true and unselfish loyalty

8. *disparaged* every attempt he made: (a) blocked, (b) supported, (c) criticized, (d) belittled

**Step 2:** *Check Up on Your Response to the Challenge*

You have here been offered a choice of possible meanings for each of the italicized words; in your own efforts, of course, you will think of one or more possibilities by yourself. As you puzzle out each word in the context in which you find it, your guesses may be correct, they may be close though not absolutely exact, or they may be far, far afield. No matter. You're working with the word, you're thinking about it, you're developing a mind-set that gives the new word an unobstructed entry into your recognition vocabulary. Having done this, your next and obvious step is to refer to a good dictionary to check up on your success in figuring out meanings. For valuable practice, make such reference to a dictionary at this very moment in respect to the eight words, to see how well you figured out their meanings. (A key to this exercise is deliberately omitted.)

**Step 3:** *Practice Pronouncing and Spelling Each Word*

Now you have the word in front of you in the

dictionary. You see its pronunciation. You are getting a second visual impression of its appearance. And you will note that it may have other forms for use as different parts of speech (adjective, noun, verb, etc.). Say the word (and any of its derivative forms) aloud. Get accustomed to hearing it in your own voice. Write the word once or twice so that you will be reacting to it muscularly as well as visually and vocally. These activities will be a giant step forward in getting on such good terms with the word that it can easily pass into your functional vocabulary and be ready for immediate use when the occasion occurs.

Do this now with our eight words. Say them aloud. Then cover each one and try spelling it correctly in the blank provided for that purpose.

1. *enervated*_____   *enervating*_____
   (to) *enervate*_____   *eneveration*_____
2. *sycophancy*_____   (a) *sycophant*_____
   *sycophantic*_____
3. *hypochondria*_____   *hypochondriacal*_____
   (a) *hypochondriac*_____
4. *introverted*_____   *introversion*_____
   (an) *introvert*_____
5. *misogyny*_____   *misogynous*_____
   *misogynistic*_____   (a) *misogynist*_____
6. *altruistic*_____   *altruism*_____
   (an) *altruist*_____
7. *anathema*_____   (to) *anathematize*_____
   *anathematization*_____
8. (to) *disparage*_____   *disparagement*_____
   *disparaging*_____

Just three simple steps to add a new word to your recognition and functional vocabulary: *keep a sharp eye open to its first appearance, and in meeting it, puzzle out a possible meaning; look it up to determine how successfully you reacted to it; then practice saying it aloud and writing it.* Do this as time and circumstances and your reading habits make possible, and you will be truly amazed at how many words will enter your vocabulary almost every day; how you will become more and more aware of their deeper meanings and various forms and uses as you continue meeting them in your reading; how you will become so familiar with them that, practically without being aware of it, you will start to use them in your thinking, your speaking, and your writing.

Do not accept these promises on faith; learn how true they are from your own experience. Here are three more exercises to make these eight words come fully alive for you, to nail them down in your vocabulary, to make them integral factors in your thinking, understanding, and self-expression.

**Exercise 1:** *True or False?*

Decide whether the following statements are substantially *true* or *false*, and check the appropriate box.

1. Staying up all night can be *enervating*.

TRUE ( )   FALSE ( )

2. *Sycophants* seek to curry favor with people of influence or wealth.   TRUE ( )   FALSE ( )

3. A *hypochondriac's* ailment can be readily discovered through a physical checkup.   TRUE ( )   FALSE ( )

4. An *introvert* is more interested in other people than in himself.   TRUE ( )   FALSE ( )

5. A *misogynist* enjoys the company of women.

TRUE ( )   FALSE ( )

6. *Altruistic* people are often well liked.

TRUE ( )   FALSE ( )

7. Communism is *anathema* to most Americans.

TRUE ( )   FALSE ( )

8. A *disparaging* remark is intended to express the speaker's praise.   TRUE ( )   FALSE ( )

KEY:   1—TRUE, 2—TRUE, 3—FALSE, 4—FALSE, 5—FALSE, 6—
TRUE, 7—TRUE, 8—FALSE

**Exercise 2:** *Same or Opposite?*

Decide whether the paired words or phrases are more
nearly the *same* or more nearly *opposed* in meaning, and
circle the appropriate letter.

| | | | |
|---|---|---|---|
| 1. enervate | strengthen | S | O |
| 2. sycophant | enemy | S | O |
| 3. hypochondriac | realist | S | O |
| 4. introvert | self-analytical person | S | O |
| 5. misogyny | love of women | S | O |
| 6. altruist | selfish person | S | O |
| 7. anathema | object of respect | S | O |
| 8. disparage | praise | S | O |

KEY:   1—O, 2—O, 3—O, 4—S, 5—O, 6—O, 7—O, 8—O.

**Exercise 3:** *What's the Word?*

Write in the appropriate blank the word which most
closely fits each definition.

1. An object of hatred                    _____
2. Tendency to analyze one's thoughts,
feelings, motives, etc.                   _____
3. To deprive of all force or strength_____
4. One who is interested in the welfare
of others                                 _____
5. Self-seeking flatterer                 _____
6. One who has imaginary ailments _____
7. To belittle; to express a low
estimate of                               _____
8. Hatred of women                        _____

KEY: 1–anathema, 2–introversion, 3–enervate, 4–altruist, 5–sycophant, 6–hypochondriac, 7–disparage, 8–
misogyny.

All right. You've seen these eight words. You've
thought about them. You've looked them up. You've
pronounced them. You've spelled them. You've reacted to them in a variety of different ways. And so
now they are yours—no one can ever take them from
you.

This has happened in perhaps only 30 minutes.

Is this good? *It is absolutely spectacular.* The average
adult who takes no active steps toward improving his
vocabulary learns at most 25 to 50 new words a year.
Yet, by following the simple and easy procedures
outlined here, you can add 8 to 14 new words (to say
nothing of the scores of derivative forms) to your
vocabulary every day you read—2000 to 3000 words
a year!

But how can you be sure to make the frequent and
repeated contacts with new words that are so essential to building a large and rich vocabulary? The
answer to this vital question will be spelled out in the
remaining pages of this chapter.

## *A READING PLAN FOR ENRICHING YOUR VOCABULARY*

Building your vocabulary effectively will involve
treating yourself to an all-around liberal education.
You will become wholly engaged and completely en-
grossed in the pursuit not only of new words but also
of *new ideas*—not only of words as symbols of information, knowledge, and understanding, but of the
*information, knowledge, and understanding itself*.

This was, curiously enough, the system by which you

operated in your childhood. During your earliest years you learned more new words, and at a faster rate, than at any other period in your life; day in and day out you squeezed every possible ounce of learning out of each waking moment, for a child has a constant and insatiable desire to know and to understand. And so, as your knowledge and your understanding increased, there was a corresponding daily increase in your store of those language symbols that described, and made it possible for you to think about and express, what you had learned.

Now that you are an adult, you have perhaps lost the strong inner drive to continue learning. If so, do not despair. You can reactivate this drive. You can recapture your former urge to know and understand, and as a direct result you can again increase your vocabulary at the same dynamic pace and in the same atmosphere of excitement that were characteristic of your childhood.

You can do this no matter what your present age or previous education.

*You can do this by exploring, through reading, new and unfamiliar fields of human knowledge, thinking, and experience.*

Below is a plan of systematic reading that will help you explore such fields—fields which will add to your vocabulary literally thousands of new, rich, meaningful, and useful words.

In each field you will find recommended the clearest and the most interesting volume available. These are not textbooks. On the contrary, they were written for the person with little or no background in the subject.

They are not necessarily easy books, yet none of them present difficulties of any major order. In combination, they offer a challenge which, when successfully met, will have a powerful effect on you. They will broaden your understanding and provide you with the words and concepts you need to express your thinking and to grasp the thoughts of others.

And this, bear in mind, is the ultimate purpose of any intelligent vocabulary building. *If words do not serve this purpose, they serve no purpose at all.*

## Recommended Readings

| Field | Book |
|---|---|
| 1. Psychology | *The Human Mind*, by Karl A. Menninger (Knopf) |
| 2. Science | *Ever Since Darwin*, by Stephen Jay Gould (Norton) |
| 3. Semantics | *Language in Thought and Action*, by S. I. Hayakawa (Harcourt, Brace Jovanovich) |
| 4. Philosophy | *The Story of Philosophy*, by Will Durant (Washington Square Press) |
| 5. Art and Music | *The Arts*, by Hendrik Willem van Loon (Liveright) |
| 6. Mathematics | *Mathematics for the Million*, by Lancelot Hogben (Norton) |

These six books will provide a point of departure. Each is, in its own field, a quick survey course. Together they are the core of a liberal-arts education.

When you have finished these volumes, you will have a running acquaintance with the general content of several vital fields of human knowledge. You will be ready to take another step in attaining a vocabulary that contains the tools for clear thinking and expression.

This step involves *specialization* in various branches of one or more fields that particularly intrigue you. Your own interests, as they develop from your survey reading, will dictate your choice of titles in each field. On pages 72 and 73 is a list of suggestions to guide you, and the abundant bibliographies contained in most survey volumes will serve as added guides. But feel free to make excursions down any side road of knowledge that your newly awakened interests may suggest.

## REMAIN ON THE ALERT FOR NEW WORDS

There will come a time, as you continue your explorations, when you discover that reading not only powerfully satisfies the urge to learn, but offers unique pleasures and mental stimulation.

You will then be impelled to strike out into new realms of reading. If previously you had read little, or had read only the lightest sort of material, you will find that reading has now become an enjoyable habit. And so you will begin to turn, for pure reading enjoyment, to the deeper and more significant novels; you will seek out general books and magazines that are addressed to the literate, discriminating, and thoughtful reader. The quantity of your reading will become considerably greater, its character much more varied, and its quality infinitely more mature and therefore infinitely more gratifying.

Turning to such reading will be an indication of your renewed intellectual growth, of a recaptured desire to reach out mentally and push back your horizons of thinking and understanding. And your new kind of reading will offer a rich source of valuable words—words of deeper, subtler, and more complex meaning than those you perhaps had previously been familiar with or accustomed to using.

Because you will have developed the habit of being alert and receptive to new words, of reacting to them, of looking them up in a dictionary, of working with them and thinking about them, a strange and wonderful thing will happen. A word which you have looked up, which you have said aloud and have actually put down in writing, will begin to appear over and over again in your varied reading—*not because it has suddenly become popular with authors, but because you have let it register deeply in your mind*. You have become strongly aware of its existence, and you are, without consciously realizing it, sharply alerted to the next appearance of the word in print.

Each succeeding time you meet this word in a different context, its meaning will become clearer, its use more familiar—until finally it will be an old friend and you will find yourself using it naturally and correctly in your speaking and writing.

This is the way new words enter fully, actively, and permanently into your vocabulary.

## LISTEN FOR NEW WORDS

There is yet another source of material for building your vocabulary.

That source is the people around you.

If you actively *look* for new words, you will be amazed at how many you will find.

If you actively *listen* for new words, you will be equally amazed at how many you will hear.

But you must become as alert and as receptive in your listening as in your looking. Does someone you are speaking to use a word you have not heard before, or a word whose meaning is not completely clear to you? *Ask about it!* Have no reluctance, feel no shame in saying, forthrightly and immediately, *"What does that word mean?"* Anyone is flattered when such a question is posed. He will be eager and happy to attempt an answer—and you may not only learn a new word but often be on the trail of a new idea, a new bit of information or knowledge.

Do you play Scrabble, Keyword, Ghost, or similar games? These are excellent vocabulary builders if you remain on the alert for new words; if you ask, when a player offers an unfamiliar term, *"What does that word means?"* and listen attentively to his answer.

## A LIFELONG PROCESS

How long will it take you to build your word stock to full strength? The process of vocabulary improvement, since it is a by-product of learning and of intellectual growth, need never end; you can be engaged in the exciting and rewarding activities outlined in this chapter for the rest of your life.

But the dividends will accrue from the moment you begin—your vocabulary will start increasing, at a spectacular rate, from the day you take your first step.

The words, and the ideas and knowledge that words symbolize, are all there. You have only to develop the habit of actively hunting for them.

## Additional Recommended Reading

*I. For specialization in various fields*

1. PSYCHOLOGY: *Cognitive Therapy & The Emotional Disorders*, by Aaron T. Beck (Meridian); *I'm O.K., You're O.K.*, by Thomas A. Harris (Avon).
2. SCIENCE: *Ascent of Man*, by Jacob Bronowski (Little, Brown); *The Sea Around Us*, by Rachel Carson (Oxford); *Red Giants & White Dwarfs*, by Robert Jastrow (Norton); *The ABC of Relativity*, by Bertrand Russell (Mentor); *The Lives of a Cell: Notes of a Biology Watcher*, by Lewis Thomas (Bantam); *The Double Helix*, by James D. Watson (Mentor).

3. SEMANTICS: *The Power of Words*, by Stuart Chase (Harcourt Brace Jovanovich); *The American Language: An Inquiry into the Development of English in the United States*, by H. L. Mencken, abr. 4th edition, Raven I. McDavid, Jr., ed. (Knopf).

4. PHILOSOPHY: *Against the Current: Essays in the History of Ideas*, by Isaiah Berlin, Henry Hardy, ed. (Penguin); *Pleasures of Philosophy*, by Will Durant (Simon and Schuster).

5. ART AND MUSIC: *The Story of Art*, by E. H. Gombrich (Prentice-Hall); *Lust for Life*, by Irving Stone (Doubleday); *What to Listen for in Music*, by Aaron Copeland (Mentor).

6. MATHEMATICS: *One, Two, Three . . . INFINITY*, by George Gamow (Bantam).

## II. Magazines for the general reader

*The Atlantic Monthly; Harper's Magazine; Natural History; Newsweek; The New Yorker; Psychology Today; Time.*

## III. Dictionaries

*Webster's New World Dictionary: Modern Desk Edition* (Collins); *Webster's Ninth New Collegiate Dictionary* (Merriam-Webster); *Random House College Dictionary* (Random House); *American Heritage Dictionary, New College Edition* (Houghton Mifflin).

# *Eleventh Day*

## THE ROYAL ROAD TO LEARNING NEW WORDS

If you work from Latin and Greek roots you can add new words to your vocabulary in wholesale quantities!

One of the quickest, surest, and most permanent methods of increasing your vocabulary is to study groups of words containing a common root.

For example, Latin *pedis* means *foot*, and as a root is spelled *ped-* in such words as *pedestrian* (someone who goes on *foot*, or, as the joke goes, a motorist who has finally found a parking place); *pedal* (a lever controlled by the *foot*); and *pedestal* (the *foot* or base of a column or statue). Knowing that the English syllable *ped-* has some relationship to *foot*, you can easily understand, and even more easily remember, the following important words:

**biped** A creature with two *feet*. Man is a *biped;* birds are also *bipeds*.
▶So the root *bi-* must mean *two*, as also in *bicycle*, a *two*-wheeled vehicle.
**quadruped** A creature with four *feet*. Dogs, cats, lions, tigers, and most other mammals are *quadrupeds*.

▶So the root *quadr-* must mean *four*, as also in *quadrilateral*, a geometric figures with *four* sides.

**impede** To hinder the progress of, get in the way of.

**impediment** A hindrance or obstruction, something that gets in the way of progress. A speech *impediment*, such as a stammer or stutter, gets in the way of fluency, almost as if one spoke with one's *foot* in one's mouth!

▶Thus, to *impede* is to tangle up someone's *feet* so that progress is difficult or impossible.

**expedite** The opposite of *impede*, this verb means to speed or facilitate the progress of: the road was widened to *expedite* traffic.

▶To *expedite* is, therefore, to free the *feet* for easy and rapid progress.

**expeditious** Rapid, prompt, without delay: the *expeditious* movements of goods and mail by airplane.


## ANOTHER WAY OF SAYING "FOOT"


*Biped, quadruped, impede,* and *expedite* are all built on the root *ped-*, from Latin *pedis, foot.* The Greeks also had a word for *foot: podis,* which occurs in English words as the root *pod-.* Consider, for example:

**podiatrist** One who treats *foot* ailments, such as corns, calluses, fallen arches. The specialty is *podiatry.*

▶Here we meet another new root, *iatr-, medical treatment. Podiatrists* are specialists in the *medical treatment* of *feet*, just as *psychiatrists* specialize in the *medical treatment* of the *psyche*, or mind.

**chiropodist** This is an older term for *podiatrist*, the latter being the official designation. Most foot doctors put both titles on their shingles, and the two words have exactly the same meaning. The specialty is *chiropody.*

▶*Chiropodist* combines *pod-, foot,* with the Greek *chiro-, hand*; in earlier days, this therapist treated hands as well as feet.

**podium** A raised platform for a speaker or orchestra conductor.

▶Thus, a *podium* is a base, or *foot*, on which to stand.

**tripod** Any support with three legs (or *feet*), as for a camera.

▶So *tri-* means *three*, as in *triangle* (a geometric figure with *three* angles), just as *bi-* means *two* and *quadr-* means *four*.

## TEST YOUR LEARNING

Notice how simple it is to understand, and how effectively (and *expeditiously!*) you can remember, the words we have discussed when you see clearly how each one is built on the root *ped-* or *pod-*, when you sense the idea of "footness" in all of them. Now, to make these words a useful part of your vocabulary, to really nail them down as permanent acquisitions, try the exercises that follow.

### 1. Say the Words

The first, and the most fruitful, step you can take in adding a word to your vocabulary is to understand, by knowing its root, why it means what it does. The next step is to become used to it, to get on relaxed and friendly terms with it by hearing it in your own voice. So say each word aloud, not once but several times, following carefully the phonetic spelling. In this way you not only make friends with a new word, but you also feel so at ease with it that it will pop up in your thinking and conversation without any conscious effort on your part.

[The symbol ə indicates the very slight vowel sound

heard in the first syllable of *commit* (kə-MIT′) or the last syllable of *Linda* (LIN′-də). The accent mark (′) shows stress, capitalized syllables receiving a stronger stress than those in lower case.]

|  |  |  |
|---|---|---|
| 1. | biped | BY′-ped |
| 2. | quadruped | KWAHD′-rōō-ped |
| 3. | impede | im-PEED′ |
| 4. | impediment | im-PED′-ə-mənt |
| 5. | expedite | EKS′-pə-dite |
| 6. | expeditious | eks′-pə-DISH′-əs |
| 7. | podiatrist | pə-DY′-ə-trist |
| 8. | chiropodist | kə-ROP′-ə-dist |
| 9. | podium | PO′-dee-əm |
| 10. | tripod | TRY′-pod |

## 2. Think with the Words

You understand these words, you're comfortable saying them, so now you're ready to start thinking with them. (And bear in mind that every word you learn or become more thoroughly acquainted with is an added tool for thinking.)

Definitions are in Column I below, words in Column II. Write the identifying letter of each word to the left of its meaning.

| | I | II |
|---|---|---|
| _____ | 1. official designation for a foot doctor | (a) biped |
| _____ | 2. older term for a foot doctor | (b) quadruped |
| _____ | 3. two-footed creature | (c) impede |
| _____ | 4. speaker's stand | (d) impediment |
| _____ | 5. four-footed creature | (e) expedite |
| _____ | 6. to make easier or quicker | (f) expeditious |
| _____ | 7. three-legged stand | (g) podiatrist |

_____8. to get in the way of      (h) chiropodist

_____9. without delay           (i) podium

_____10. obstruction           (j) tripod

KEY:   1–g, 2–h, 3–a, 4–i, 5–b, 6–e, 7–j, 8–c, 9–f, 10–d.

## 3. Use the Words

You understand the words, you've said them, you've thought about them. Now can you use them when you need them? Write in the blank the word we've studied that meaningfully completes each sentence.

1. A camera is often mounted on a _____.

2. Unlike most other mammals, man is a _____.

3. But a wolf, cow, or horse is a _____.

4. A foot doctor is called either a _____ or _____.

5. Narrow roads and frequent stoplights usually _____ the rapid flow of traffic.

6. And so most states are building wide, limited-access highways to _____ traffic.

7. Military roads are built to accommodate the _____ movement of troops and vehicles.

8. A speaker generally delivers his address from a _____.

9. His unpleasant personality acts, unfortunately, as a great _____ to his advancement in the company.

KEY:   1–tripod, 2–biped, 3–quadruped, 4–chiropodist/podiatrist, 5–impede, 6–expedite, 7–expeditious, 8–podium, 9–impediment.

## 4. Remember the Roots

The roots you have learned have brought you to a quick understanding of ten valuable words. As you will realize shortly, these same roots can unlock for you the meaning of scores of additional new words you may meet in your reading or hear in conversation. Are you sure you have these roots straight? Then correctly match the two columns.

| *Root* | *Meaning* |
|---|---|
| _____1. *ped-* | (a) three |
| _____2. *bi-* | (b) two |
| _____3. *quadr-* | (c) foot |
| _____4. *pod-* | (d) medical treatment |
| _____5. *iatr-* | (e) hand |
| _____6. *psych-* | (f) four |
| _____7. *chiro-* | (g) mind |
| _____8. *tri-* | |

KEY: 1–c, 2–b, 3–f, 4–c, 5–d, 6–g, 7–e, 8–a.

## ANOTHER KIND OF "PED-"

There is no more effective means of learning new words quickly, permanently, and in wholesale quantities than by seeing how they occur in related families. By examining the *ped* and *pod-* families, you have, in a few minutes, made a strong and lasting contact with ten valuable words and, in addition, have learned six useful new roots. Now let us look at another *ped-* family, one that comes to us not from Latin *pedis* but from Greek *paidos*.

Greek *paidos* means *child*. In English words built on *paidos*, the root is again spelled *ped-*, though this syllable has no relation, despite its identical appearance, to Latin *ped-*, *foot*. For example:

**pediatrics** The medical specialty of *children's* diseases. The doctor is a *pediatrician*.

▶Once again, our friend *iatr-*, *medical treatment*.

**pedagogy** The science, art, or principles of teaching.

▶This word combines *paidos, child*, with the Greek noun *agogos*, leader, from the verb *agein*, to lead—hence . . . *children*.

**pedagogue** A teacher, usually one who is stuffy, excessively precise, or dogmatic.

▶The word is not a bit complimentary and indicates our irritation with teachers who flaunt their learning in correcting our errors.

**orthopedics** The medical specialty dealing with bones and joints. Broken legs, curvature of the spine, club foot, and other skeletal injuries or deformities are the province of the *orthopedist* or *orthopedic surgeon*.

▶This word combines *padios, child*, and the root *ortho-, straight* or *correct*, the idea being that a child's bones are more pliable and hence more easily straightened, corrected, or mended than those of an adult, though of course an *orthopedist* does not by any means limit his practice to children.

## *NEW ROOTS LEAD TO NEW WORDS*

Building your vocabulary through an exploration of word roots is not only amazingly simple, rapid, and effective, but also remarkably productive. An excursion into one family of words automatically turns up new families that promise endless and exciting discoveries, as you have already seen.

Starting with Latin *pedis*, you were soon involved with Greek *podis* and *paidos*. You learned, or became reacquainted with, a score of vital, useful words and discovered new roots that unlocked still more words to add to your vocabulary.

Suppose, therefore, we continue the process of letting roots lead to new words, which in turn lead to new roots, which in turn . . . etc., by looking once again at *bi-*.

1. *bi-* means *two*.

**bigamy** *Two* marriages. The *bigamist* takes a second wife or husband while a previous union is still in effect. The adjective is *bigamous*.

▶So *gam-* must mean *marriage*. Let us see what interesting words this new root leads us to.

2. *gam-* means *marriage*.

**monogamy** The system of only one *marriage* at a time. The adjective is *monogamous*.

▶ So *mon-* must mean *one*, as in *monocle*, a lens for *one* eye, and *monarch*, the *one* supreme ruler of a nation. Knowing the meaning of *mon-*, can you figure out *monologue, monotheism, monosyllable?*

**polygamy** The custom permitting a man many wives (or *marriages*), once practiced by the Mormons in Utah. The adjective is *polygamous*.

▶So *poly-* must mean *many*, as in *polygon*, a geometric figure of *many* sides. Can you, then, figure out *polysyllable, polyglot* (*glot-* means *tongue* or *language*), *polytheism* (*theos* means *god*)?

**misogamy** The hatred of *marriage*. The adjective is *misogamous;* the hater is a *misogamist*.

▶So *mis-* (from Greek *misein*) must mean *hatred*.

3. *mis-* (Greek *misein*) means *hatred*.

**misanthropy** The *hatred* of all mankind. The person who hates everyone is a *misanthrope*. The adjective is *misanthropic*.

▶So *anthrop-* must mean *mankind*, as in *anthropology*, the science of mankind's development, and *philanthropy*, the love of *mankind* (*phil-* means *love*).

**misogyny** The *hatred* of women. A *misogynist* hates all females, usually for dark reasons that only a psychiatrist can unravel. The adjective is *misogynous*.

▶So *gyn-* must mean *woman*, as in *gynecology*, the medical study of ailments peculiar to *women*.

Let us pause now and consolidate our recent discoveries.

## TEST YOUR LEARNING

### 1. Say the Words

Pronounce each word aloud several times.

| | | |
|---|---|---|
| 1. | pediatrics | pee-dee-AT'-riks |
| 2. | pedagogy | PED'-ə-gō'-jee |
| 3. | pedagogue | PED'-ə-gog |
| 4. | orthopedics | awr'-thə-PEE'-diks |
| 5. | bigamy | BIG'-ə-mee |
| 6. | monogamy | mə-NOG'-ə-mee |
| 7. | polygamy | pə-LIG'-ə-mee |
| 8. | misogamy | mə-SOG'-ə-mee |
| 9. | misanthropy | mə-SAN'-thrə-pee |
| 10. | misogyny | mə-SOJ'-ə-nee |

### 2. Think with the Words

Match the columns.

| I | II |
|---|---|
| \_\_\_\_\_1. hatred of women | (a) pediatrics |
| \_\_\_\_\_2. one marriage at a time | (b) pedagogy |
| \_\_\_\_\_3. a "schoolmarmish" teacher | (c) pedagogue |
| \_\_\_\_\_4. specialty of children's diseases | (d) orthopedic |
| | (e) bigamy |
| \_\_\_\_\_5. plurality of wives | (f) monogamy |
| \_\_\_\_\_6. art of teaching | (g) polygamy |
| \_\_\_\_\_7. crime of additional marriage without divorce, annulment, etc. | (h) misogamy |
| \_\_\_\_\_8. hatred of all mankind | |

_____9. medical treatment of skele-    (i) misanthropy
      tal injuries or deformities    (j) misogyny

_____10. hatred of marriage

KEY:   1–j, 2–f, 3–c, 4–a, 5–g, 6–b, 7–e, 8–i, 9–d, 10–h.

## 3. Use the Words

Fill in the blanks to make meaningful sentences. Forms of the words other than those in the pronunciation list may sometimes be required—as *pediatrician, orthopedist*, etc.

1. A _____ shuns females—love for them is beyond his capacity.

2. The specialist who sets bone fractures is known as an _____.

3. Mothers usually take their new infants to a _____ for a medical check-up.

4. One husband, one wife—this is the system known as _____.

5. If a sailor has a wife in every port, he is a _____.

6. Those preparing to teach take college courses in _____.

7. The hatred of a _____ is directed against the entire human race.

8. _____ is no longer sanctioned in this country, but at one time was practiced by the Mormons.

9. There are those who direct their hatred against institutions instead of people—a \_\_\_ _____, for example, hates marriage.

10. A stuffy, straitlaced teacher is often referred to, derogatively, as a _____.

KEY:   1–misogynist, 2–orthopedist (*or* orthopedic surgeon), 3–pediatrician, 4–monogamy, 5–bigamist, 6–pedagogy, 7–misanthrope, 8–polygamy, 9–misogamist, 10–pedagogue.

## 4. Remember the Roots

Match roots and meanings.

| Root |     |      | Meaning |                  |
|------|-----|------|---------|------------------|
|      | 1.  | *paidos*   | (a) | one              |
|      | 2.  | *agogos*   | (b) | god              |
|      | 3.  | *ortho-*   | (c) | mankind          |
|      | 4.  | *gam-*     | (d) | woman            |
|      | 5.  | *mon-*     | (e) | love             |
|      | 6.  | *poly-*    | (f) | child            |
|      | 7.  | *mis-*     | (g) | marriage         |
|      | 8.  | *anthrop-* | (h) | tongue, language |
|      | 9.  | *phil-*    | (i) | straight, correct|
|      | 10. | *gyn-*     | (j) | to lead          |
|      | 11. | *glot-*    | (k) | hatred           |
|      | 12. | *theos*    | (l) | many             |

KEY: 1–f, 2–j, 3–i, 4–g, 5–a, 6–l, 7–k, 8–c, 9–e, 10–d, 11–h, 12–b.

## *A FEW ROOTS UNLOCK THE SECRETS OF HUNDREDS OF WORDS*

So far we have made contact with 20 extremely productive Latin and Greek roots and intensively studied 20 English words and some of their derivative forms. In our quick excursions into roots, however, we noticed in passing another 20 or so words, many of them perhaps quite new to you—and yet we have hardly begun to tap the rich resources of the roots we've uncovered.

You can take the most complex words, and any number of them, and if you can recognize the roots on which they're built you will have no difficulty understanding them, remembering them, and keeping them unconfused in your mind. By becoming familiar with the common roots we've discussed, you have taken a giant step forward in building a larger and more meaningful vocabulary, *for you are now able to figure out hundreds of words that you may never have seen or heard of before.*

So at this point let us take another quick look at some of the roots we've been working with and see how easy it is to discover 27 additional words, even though we'll hardly do much more than scratch the surface of the possibilities.

Doesn't recognizing the root in the following words make them immediately understandable and almost absurdly simple to remember?

1. *ped-* means *foot*

**centipede** A wormlike creature that seems to have a hundred *feet*, which is, of course, an exaggeration.

**velocipede** A child's tricycle propelled by speedy *feet*.

2. *bi-* means *two*

**bisect** To cut into *two* equal parts.

**bilingual** Able to speak *two* languages.

**biennial** Every *two* years.

**bilateral** Having, or involving, *two* sides.

3. *tri-* means *three*

**triplets** *Three* children at a single birth.

**trisect** To cut into *three* equal parts.

**trilingual** Able to speak *three* languages.

**triennial** Every *three* years.

4. *quadr-* means *four*

**quadruplets** *Four* children at a single birth.

**quadrennial** Every *four* years.

**quadrisyllable** A word of *four* syllables.

5. *ortho-* means *straight, correct*

**orthodontia** The branch of dentistry dealing with *straightening* the teeth, *correcting* the bite, etc.

**orthography** *Correct* writing, hence the system of spelling a language.

6. *agogos* means *leader*

**demagogue** One who pretends to be a *leader* of the people but in actuality foments discontent among the masses in order to gain power.

**synagogue** Jewish temple in which people are *led* or brought together to worship God.

7. *anthrop-* means *mankind*

**anthropoid** Similar to *man* in form or appearance, as the *anthropoid* apes.

8. *theos* means *god*

**theology** The study of *God* or religion

**monotheism** Belief in one *God*.

**atheism** Complete disbelief in the existence of *God*.

9. *phil-* means *love*

**Philadelphia** The city of brotherly *love*.

**philology** The *love* of words, hence the science of language.

**philter** A *love* potion.

**philander** To make *love* trifingly and insincerely.

**bibliophile** One who *loves* books; also, a collector of books.

**philatelist** A stamp collector; one who *loves* stamps.

Some of these words are commonly mispronounced. To give you greater assurance in using them, practice aloud the pronunciations given below.

| | |
|---|---|
| velocipede | və-LOS'-ə-peed |
| orthodontia | awr'-thə-DON'-shə |
| orthography | awr-THOG'-rə-fee |
| demagogue | DEM'-ə-gog |
| theology | thee-OL'-ə-jee |
| monotheism | MON'-ə-thee-iz-əm |
| atheism | AY'-thee-iz-əm |

| philology | fə-LOL'-ə-jee |
| philander | fə-LAN'-dər |
| bibliophile | BIB'-lee-ə-file |
| philatelist | fə-LAT'-ə-list |

## LET'S TIE IT ALL UP

In the short time it took you to cover the material in this chapter you have either learned for the first time, or become reacquainted with on a deeper level, approximately 67 expressive and highly useful English words—more than the average adult learns in two years. More important, you have come to realize that words, like people, grow in families, and that the parent in these families is often a Greek or Latin root.

When you have control of a root you are in command of scores of words, you can figure out the meanings of words you may never have seen before, you understand words more fully, you know why a word means what it does.

And from now on you will probably note a curious phenomenon. The words you have studied today will begin to appear over and over again in your reading—not because they have suddenly become popular, but because you have an understanding of them that will make them doubly conspicuous, and considerably more meaningful, every time you meet them.

*Very soon, and this you will shortly discover for yourself, you will begin to use these new words—and without hesitation or self-consciousness.*

So now, to wrap it all up in a neat little package, are you ready to try a simple test on the word roots we've studied? Here are 20 of our words chosen at random from the 67 we've worked with. In each, a single root is italicized. Can you write the English meaning of each *root* in the blank provided?

1. ex*ped*itious_____
2. *ped*agogy_____
3. *mono*gamy_____
4. poly*glot*_____
5. *miso*gyny_____
6. ped*iatrics*_____
7. *pod*iatry_____
8. *bi*lingual_____
9. *tri*ennial_____
10. *chiro*podist_____
11. dem*agogue*_____
12. mis*anthrop*y_____
13. *poly*theism_____
14. *phil*anthropy_____
15. *ortho*pedics_____
16. *theo*logy_____
17. *quadr*uped_____
18. *psych*iatry_____
19. poly*gamy*_____
20. *gyn*ecology_____

KEY:  1—foot, 2—child, 3—one, 4—tongue, language, 5—hatred, 6—medical treatment, 7—foot, 8—two, 9—three, 10—hand, 11—to lead, 12—mankind, 13—many, 14—love, 15—straight, correct, 16—god, 17—four, 18—mind, 19—marriage, 20—woman.

# *Twelfth Day*

## LET'S LEARN TEN NEW WORDS

A quick warm-up that will help you add some short and expressive terms to your vocabulary.

Do you have a good stock of short, graphic terms with which to express your ideas? Complete as many of the following words as you can, then add to your vocabulary by studying the key that follows the test.

| | | |
|---|---|---|
| 1. | dark, grayish-blue in color | L_____ID |
| 2. | heated or vehement in spirit | F_____ID |
| 3. | extreme in opinion or practice | R_____ID |
| 4. | wan; without color | P_____ID |
| 5. | clear; easily understood | L_____ID |
| 6. | diseased; gruesome; easily influenced by ideas of a gloomy nature | M_____ID |
| 7. | filthy; dirty; mean | S_____ID |
| 8. | frank; honest; truthful | C_____ID |
| 9. | bright; sharp; clear | V_____ID |
| 10. | glaringly sensational; marked by violent passion or crime | L_____ID |

1. Livid. This can best be understood by thinking of a black-and-blue bruise. Also used figuratively, as *livid with rage*, when the face takes on this unpleasant color.

2. Fervid. A *fervid* attitude is ardent and zealous; a *fervid* attack is warm and passionate. This word comes from a Latin verb meaning *to boil* or *flame*.

3. Rabid. A *rabid* person is fanatical, goes to extreme lengths in expressing an opinion or taking a stand. This word is from a Latin stem meaning *to rave*, the same stem from which we derive *rabies*, the disease that affects dogs.

4. Pallid. This word is essentially similar in meaning to pale, except for its added implication that color or health has been lost through some abnormal condition such as weakness, illness, fainting, fatigue, etc.

5. Lucid. If anything is *lucid*, it is clear or easy to understand. We may speak of *lucid* prose, a *lucid* argument, or of a mental patient whose mind is no longer *lucid*.

6. Morbid. In its medical sense, *morbid* implies lack of health, as in a *morbid* condition of the lungs or a *morbid* growth on the intestines; in its extended and more general meaning, the word implies unnatural gruesomeness or gloomy pessimism, as in the *morbid* cartoons of Charles Addams or the *morbid* atmosphere of Russian novels. The word derives from Latin *morbus*, disease.

7. Sordid. This is a difficult word to explain because so much of its impact comes from its emotional flavor rather than from its direct meaning. A *sordid* atmosphere implies repulsiveness and degradation, lack of cleanliness and cheerfulness, perhaps even an open display of base passions or immorality. *Sordid* surroundings might be mean, dirty, indicative of dire poverty. A *sordid* book might deal with vile people and foul doings. The word comes from Latin *sordere*, to be dirty.

8. Candid. A *candid* person is frank, aboveboard, not given to deception or concealment. If you are noted for your *candidness*, you do not attempt to hide what you know, even at the risk of hurting people's feelings or putting yourself at a disadvantage. The word is from

Latin *toga candidus*, the white (for purity) garment worn by Roman office-seekers who thereby signified that they had nothing to conceal—and it is from the same root that we get the word *candidate*.

9. Vivid. A *vivid* picture is sharp and clear; *vivid* colors are brilliant, like bright red or green, rather than dull, like gray or black; a *vivid* account appeals powerfully to the imagination, has a sharp impact on the emotions, etc. The word is from the Latin *vivere*, to be alive.

10. Lurid. A woman with a *lurid* past has lived sensationally, notoriously, scandalously; the *lurid* details of death, catastrophe, etc., are those which might offend the sensitive reader or listener—such extreme details might be excessively gruesome, repugnant, or disgusting.

# *Thirteenth Day*

## A CHALLENGE TO YOUR VOCABULARY

---

Here are 50 more words that should be in every educated person's vocabulary—how successfully can *you* learn them?

---

A test can be used for one of two purposes: to check on your knowledge, or to motivate your learning. These tests have the latter end in view.

It is true in a sense that if you cannot answer a question you thereby display your ignorance. It is equally true, and far more important, that when you finally discover the correct answer to the question you thereupon erase that ignorance.

In the five tests which follow, you will be asked 50 questions—*and your learning will come from the questions you cannot answer.* Each test will take you no more than three minutes. Go through the tests quickly, guessing as wildly as you like; then pay particular attention to the answers. For every mistake you make you will learn a new word. The more errors, the more words you will add to your vocabulary. So have no fear of coming through with a low score—the lower it is, the greater you gain!

**Test 1:** *People*

1. Are babies delivered by (a) *a pediatrician*, (b) *an osteopath*, or (c) *an obstetrician*?

2. Are teeth straightened by (a) *an orthodontist*, (b) *a podiatrist*, or (c) *an orthopedist*?

3. Is music played superbly by (a) *a chanteuse*, (b) *a tyro*, or (c) *a virtuoso*?

4. Is a loud-mouthed, turbulent woman (a) *a feminist*, (b) *a virago*, or (c) *an executrix*?

5. Is a politician who tries to cause unrest among the masses so he may gain his own selfish ends (a) *a reactionary*, (b) *a demagogue*, or (c) *a radical*?

6. Is someone who arranges a ballet (a) *a choreographer*, (b) *a thespian*, or (c) *a terpsichorean*?

7. Is a doctor who performs eye surgery (a) *an ophthalmologist*, (b) *an optician*, or (c) *an optometrist*?

8. Is someone who dabbles in the arts (a) *a gourmet*, (b) *a connoisseur*, or (c) *a dilettante*?

9. Is someone who has dedicated his life to beauty (a) *a voluptuary*, (b) *an aesthete*, or (c) *an ascetic*?

10. Is a stamp collector (a) *a bibliophile*, (b) *a numismatist*, or (c) *a philatelist*?

KEY:  1–c, 2–a, 3–c, 4–b, 5–b, 6–a, 7–a, 8–c, 9–b, 10–c.

**Test:** *The Sciences*

1. Does *anthropology* deal with the development of (a) plants, (b) animals, or (c) mankind?

2. Is *astronomy* concerned with (a) rocks, (b) stars, or (c) insects?

3. Does *semantics* explore (a) the meanings of words, (b) the source of words, or (c) the use of words?

4. Does *entomology* deal with (a) words, (b) insects, or (c) fish?

5. Does *etymology* deal with (a) words, (b) insects, or (c) fish?

6. Is *eugenics* the science of (a) social conditions, (b) better offspring, or (c) atomic energy?

7. Does *dermatology* relate to diseases of the (a) digestive tract, (b) skin. or (c) feet?

8. Is *ornithology* concerned with (a) birds, (b) reptiles, or (c) climate?

9. Does *geriatrics* attempt to solve the problems of (a) infancy, (b) adolescence, or (c) old age?

10. Is *genetics* interested in (a) heredity, (b) conservation, or (c) mineral resources?

KEY:   1–c, 2–b, 3–a, 4–b, 5–a, 6–b, 7–b, 8–a, 9–c, 10–a.

**Test 3:** *Abnormal States*

|  | YES | NO |
|---|---|---|
| 1. Does *amnesia* mean loss of memory? | | |
| 2. Does *aphasia* affect the ability to walk? | | |
| 3. Does a *somnambulist* walk in his sleep? | | |
| 4. Does *insomnia* keep one up at night? | | |
| 5. Is a *neurosis* more serious than a *psychosis*? | | |
| 6. Is *claustrophobia* fear of open spaces? | | |
| 7. Is *dipsomania* related to thievery? | | |
| 8. Is *acrophobia* fear of high places? | | |
| 9. Is *egocentricity* a morbid interest in oneself? | | |
| 10. Is *pyromania* related to fire? | | |

KEY:   1–Yes; 2–No, *aphasia* is loss of impairment of the ability to use language; 3–Yes; 4–Yes; 5–No, a *neurosis* is an emotional disorder caused by conflicts, tensions, insecurity, etc., but a *psychosis* is a severe form of mental derangement; 6—No, *claustrophobia* is morbid fear of enclosed spaces, *agoraphobia* is fear of open places; 7—No, *dipsomania* is another name for alcoholism, *kleptomania* is related to thievery; 8—Yes; 9—Yes; 10—Yes, the *pyromaniac* has a morbid and irresistible compulsion to set fires.

**Test 4:** *Actions*

|  | TRUE | FALSE |
|---|---|---|
| 1. *Verify* means to ascertain the truth of something. | —— | —— |
| 2. *Soliloquize* means to think silently about something. | —— | —— |
| 3. To *alleviate* means to aggravate, make worse. | —— | —— |
| 4. To *deprecate* is to belittle. | —— | —— |
| 5. To *cower* is to stand up bravely to danger. | —— | —— |
| 6. To *cavil* is to raise trivial objections. | —— | —— |
| 7. To *badger* is to torment, annoy, harass. | —— | —— |
| 8. If you *temporize*, you meet your obligations promptly. | —— | —— |
| 9. To *meander* is to wander aimlessly. | —— | —— |
| 10. To *malign* someone is to recommend him heartily. | —— | —— |

KEY: 1—True; 2—False, it means to talk aloud to oneself; 3—False, it means to diminish or lessen; 4—True; 5—False, to *cower* is to crouch in fear; 6—True; 7—True; 8—False, if you *temporize* you play for time, postpone, or procrastinate; 9—True; 10—False, to *malign* someone is to slander him.

**Test 5:** *Comparisons*

|  | SAME | OPPOSITE |
|---|---|---|
| 1. Do *parsimonious* and *prodigal* mean the same or opposite? | _____ | _____ |
| 2. Are *aquiline* and *straight* the same or opposite? | _____ | _____ |
| 3. Are *taciturn* and *loquacious* the same or opposite? | _____ | _____ |
| 4. Are *exigency* and *emergency* the same or opposite? | _____ | _____ |
| 5. Do *enervated* and *exhausted* mean the same or opposite? | _____ | _____ |
| 6. Are *erudite* and *ignorant* the same or opposite? | _____ | _____ |
| 7. Are *apathetic* and *lethargic* the same or opposite? | _____ | _____ |
| 8. Do *savor* and *flavor* mean the same or opposite? | _____ | _____ |
| 9. Are *inclement* and *mild* the same or opposite? | _____ | _____ |
| 10. Are *coquetry* and *flirtatiousness* the same or opposite? | _____ | _____ |

KEY:　1—opposite: *parsimonious* is stingy, *prodigal* is extravagant; 2—opposite: *aquiline* means beaked, curved; 3—opposite: *taciturn* means quiet, disinclined to talk, *loquacious* means talkative; 4—same; 5—same; 6—opposite: *erudite* means learned; 7—same; both words mean *having or exhibiting little or no feeling;* 8—same; 9—opposite: *inclement* means harsh, unfavorable; 10—same.

## TEST YOUR LEARNING

Now, to show you how easy it is to add to your vocabulary, let me offer you a quick test designed to check your learning. Spend a little time examining your mistakes, if any, and let the correct answers erase such areas of ignorance as the original test may have revealed. Then, when you are ready, take this last test.

*Directions:* Write one of the words discussed in these pages which best fits the brief definition. The initial letter is offered to guide your thinking.

1. first assistant to the stork    o_____
2. accomplished musician    v_____
3. arranger of the ballet    c_____
4. devotee of beauty    a_____
5. science of heavenly bodies    a_____
6. study of insects    e_____
7. study of heredity    g_____
8. science that deals with the problems of old age    g_____
9. loss of memory    a_____
10. loss of power to use language    a_____
11. alcoholism    d_____
12. fear of restricted areas    c_____
13. to speak aloud to oneself    s_____
14. to lessen    a_____
15. to crouch in fear    c_____
16. to slander, or gossip about, someone    m_____
17. tight-fisted    p_____
18. worn out with fatigue    e_____
19. harsh, unfavorable    i_____
20. learned, versed in book knowledge    e_____

KEY: 1—obstetrician, 2—virtuoso, 3—choreographer, 4—aesthete, 5—astronomy, 6—entomology, 7—genetics, 8—geriatrics, 9—amnesia, 10—aphasia, 11—dipsomania, 12—claustrophobia, 13—soliloquize, 14—alleviate, 15—cower, 16—malign, 17—parsimonious, 18—enervated, 19—inclement, 20—erudite.

# Fourteenth Day

## JUST FOR FUN (III)

### I. THE MISPLACED MONTHS

If you ever studied Latin, you have no doubt wondered why *September*, named after the Latin numeral *septem* (seven), stands for our *ninth* month. And why October, November, and December, respectively from the Roman numbers *octo* (eight), *novem* (nine), and *decem* (ten), actually refer to our tenth, eleventh, and twelfth months. The explanation is simple: The old Roman calendar started with March, not January, and September, October, November, and December *were* the seventh, eighth, ninth, and tenth months in early Roman times. When we revised the calendar, we slipped in two extra months at the beginning of the year but never got around to changing the four misleading names.

### II. WHAT'S WRONG WITH THIS?

*This criteria is not, in my opinion, very reliable.*
*Criteria* is a plural noun, although admittedly it has an amazing resemblance to a singular. (The singular form is *criterion*.) Hence, adjective *this* and verb *is* should also be plural. Correct form: *These criteria are not . . . reliable.*

*The alumni of Girls' High School will hold their annual meeting in April.*

Graduates of a girls' school would likely be females. *Alumni*, plural of *alumnus*, refers only to males. Correct word in the sentence offered: *alumnae*, plural of *alumna*, the feminine form of *alumnus*. Pronounce them as follows: *alumni:* ə-LUM -'nye; *alumnae:* ə-LUM -'nee.

*Why don't you lay down for a nap before dinner?*

The verb is wrong. *Lay* means to place or put. The required form, which would mean to rest or recline, is *lie*.

*I'm surprised you didn't get an invite to Charlie Jerome's party.*

*Invite* may be used only as a verb. Proper form: *invitation*.

*What an aggravating child she is!*

The original meaning of *aggravate* was *to make worse, to intensify*, and so grammarians have in the past warned against its use as a synonym for *exasperate* or *irritate*. However, words change with usage, and since *aggravating* is now widely used in both speech and writing with the meaning of *annoying*, the sentence as it stands is acceptable English.

*No one but I can help you.*

In this sentence, *but* means *except* and is a preposition. According to grammatical rule, prepositions govern the objective case of the pronoun; hence, the proper phrasing is: *No one but me can help you.*

*It is I who is responsible for this trouble.*

*Who* takes the same verb as does its antecedent. The antecedent of *who* in this sentence is *I*. Since we say *I am*, not *I is*, the sentence should read: *It is I who am responsible* . . .

*Can I borrow your pen if you're not using it?*

Purists rail against the use of *can* to seek permission, and parents from time immemorial (and with little success) have attempted to train their children to show politeness by using *may* as a substitute. Nevertheless, it is today established and cultivated usage to ask permission with the verb *can*.

   *What affect does he have on you?*

Except with a special and technical meaning in psychology, *affect* is used only as a verb. Here a noun is required. Correct form: *effect*.

   *How does he effect you?*

In this sentence a verb is required. Correct form: *affect*.


### III. HOW GOOD IS YOUR VOCABULARY?

Everybody realizes the value of a large vocabulary. There is no doubt that the better a person's verbal equipment, the more accurately he can think about and analyze life's complex problems.

Have you ever wondered how your vocabulary compares with the average? If you have, these tests will give you a reliable answer.

**Test 1:** *Is Your Vocabulary Average?*

If it is, you should be able to determine in at least 4 instances out of 5 whether word and definition are the same or opposite in meaning.

   1. *audacity; boldness*          SAME ( )   OPPOSITE ( )
   2. *incessant; never-ending*  SAME ( )   OPPOSITE ( )
   3. *adept; awkward*             SAME ( )   OPPOSITE ( )
   4. to *scoff at;* to *respect*   SAME ( )   OPPOSITE ( )
   5. *precise; accurate*           SAME ( )   OPPOSITE ( )

**Test 2:** *Is Your Vocabulary Good?*

Then you will be able to check the correct meaning of at least 4 of the following 5 words.

1. *mercenary:* (a) influenced exclusively by money; (b) commercial; (c) expensive

2. *arrogant:* (a) shy; (b) excessively proud and self-confident; (c) intelligent, possessed of a keen mind

3. *to replenish:* (a) use carefully; (b) save for future use; (c) renew, refill

4. *gourmand:* (a) ravenous eater, glutton; (b) stickler for etiquette; (c) wealthy man, plutocrat

5. *frugal:* (a) thrifty; (b) extravagant; (e) foolish

**Test 3:** *Have You an Excellent Vocabulary?*

Then you should be able to match *all* the words in the first column with their correct synonyms in the second column.

| | |
|---|---|
| 1. *crass* | (a) wealthy |
| 2. *opulent* | (b) showing off one's learning |
| 3. *nebulous* | (c) basic |
| 4. *pedantic* | (d) cruel |
| 5. *adamant* | (e) indistinct, obscure, vague |
| | (f) unyielding |
| | (g) crude |

**Test 4:** *Is Your Vocabulary Superior?*

Then you will sail right through these difficult words, choosing a proper definition in every case.

1. *contrite:* (a) remorseful; (b) irritable; (c) trustworthy

2. *vagary:* (a) rare gem; (b) wild idea, freakish whim; (c) pleasant surprise

3. *to obfuscate:* (a) misunderstand; (b) solve; (c) confuse or bewilder

4. *parsimonious:* (a) religious; (b) stingy; (c) hypocritical

5. *anathema:* (a) drug that alleviates pain; (b) philosophy of life; (c) object of deep hatred

KEY:   Test 1: 1—SAME; 2—SAME; 3—OPPOSITE; 4—OPPOSITE
    5—SAME.
    Test 2:   1–a, 2–b, 3–c, 4–a, 5–a.
    Test 3:   1–g, 2–a, 3–e, 4–b, 5–f.
    Test 4:   1–a, 2–b, 3–c, 4–b, 5–c.

# PART IV

# *Spell It Right!*

In just five days you can increase your spelling skill almost miraculously!

# *Fifteenth Day*

## SPECIAL TRICKS THAT WILL
## MAKE YOU A BETTER SPELLER

---

Learning to be a good speller may seem difficult—
but there are tested short cuts to quick and permanent
mastery of the words most people misspell.

---

### *EVERYONE HAS TROUBLE WITH SPELLING*

English spelling is, without a doubt, the most perplex-
ing, the most confounding, the most contradictory, and
the most frustrating system of putting letters together
ever devised by man.

No wonder, therefore, that few people feel any security or self-confidence about their ability to spell correctly—or that only the rare person is always sure
whether or not to double a consonant (embarassment
or embarrassment, cooly or coolly?); whether to write *ie*
or *ei* (wierd or weird, niece or neice?); whether to use
-*able* or -*ible* (irresistable or irresistible, indispensable or
indispensible?); or whether to end a word with -*ance* or
-*ence* (perseverance or perseverence, insistance or insistence?).

Nor should it be a surprise that even people who are
completely literate in every other way have trouble with

spelling. Novelist F. Scott Fitzgerald was a notoriously bad speller. So was Andrew Jackson, who, when he was twitted on his frequent errors, retorted characteristically, "Well, sir, it's a poor mind that cannot think of more than one way to spell a word!"

And yet, despite the problems caused by our out-of-date, inconsistent, and complicated spelling system, the average person is a better speller than he may realize—*for 95 percent of his errors occur in a list of about 100 fairly common words that he may use over and over again in his writing*. These are demons that seem to have, as it were, two spellings: a correct form and a popular, frequently used, but totally incorrect and unacceptable form. *And both patterns usually look equally good to the untrained speller.*

Let us put it to a test whether you have the same trouble with these words that almost everyone else has.

Below, you will find 20 of the top demons on the list, each spelled in two ways: the approved form and the common misspelling. It is up to you to decide which is which.

Consider yourself far above average if you make 9 to 13 proper choices, and a really superior speller if you score 14 or higher.

1. (a) alright, (b) all right
2. (a) supersede, (b) supercede
3. (a) embarassed, (b) embarrassed
4. (a) drunkeness, (b) drunkenness
5. (a) irresistible, (b) irresistable
6. (a) occurrance, (b) occurrence
7. (a) ecstasy, (b) ecstacy
8. (a) anoint, (b) annoint
9. (a) occassion, (b) occasion
10. (a) disappoint, (b) dissapoint
11. (a) analize, (b) analyze
12. (a) tyranny, (b) tyrrany
13. (a) inoculate, (b) inocculate

14. (a) cooly, (b) coolly
15. (a) indispensable, (b) indispensible
16. (a) superintendent, (b) superintendant
17. (a) battalion, (b) batallion
18. (a) perseverance, (b) perseverence
19. (a) iridescent, (b) irredescent
20. (a) reccomend, (b) recommend

KEY:  1–b, 2–a, 3–b, 4–b, 5–a, 6–b, 7–a, 8–a, 9–b, 10–a, 11–b, 12–a, 13–a, 14–b, 15–a, 16–a, 17–a, 18–a, 19–a, 20–b.


## HOW TO ELIMINATE YOUR TROUBLE

Yes, as you discovered from the test you have just taken, or as perhaps you knew all along, English spelling is indeed contradictory and confusing. For example, we must spell it:

pro*ceed*, but pre*cede*
s*ei*ze, but s*ie*ge
resist*ance*, but persist*ence*
indispens*able*, but irresist*ible*
dum*b*, but, preferably, dum*founded*
liqu*i*d, but liqu*e*fy
morali*ze*, but anal*yze*
dissi*p*ate, but disa*pp*oint
a*n*nounce, but a*n*oint
a*l*ready, but *all* right
prefe*r*ence, but occu*rr*ence

So if you have a sense of inadequacy about your spelling, or if you are confused more often than you are sure, take heart. Investigations have proved that *most people not only misspell the same words but misspell them in exactly the same way.*

It is this fact that makes it so easy for you to achieve a spectacular improvement in the accuracy of your spelling, as well as a considerable increase in your confidence, by spending just a few days in simple self-training. For if you fancy yourself an imperfect or even an extremely poor speller, the chances are that you have developed an inferiority complex solely because you are in doubt about most or all of the approximately 100 demons with which Part IV of this book deals. Conquer this single list of commonly misspelled words and 95 percent of your spelling difficulties will in all likelihood vanish.

### How Do You Go about It?

1. By learning to use a few simple memory-association tricks that will help you choose correct patterns, discard incorrect ones. (Such memory tricks are known technically as *mnemonics*, pronounced *nə-MON -iks*.)

2. By training both your *visual* memory (so that only the correct forms will *look* proper) and your *muscular* memory (so that you will without a moment's thought or hesitation *write* only the correct forms).

3. By thoroughly understanding how to apply half a dozen clear-cut and serviceable spelling principles that will rule out the slightest possibility of error in certain confusing groups of words.

That doesn't sound very hard, does it? Then let's begin.

### Speed!

Eleven—and only eleven—words in our language containing more than one syllable terminate with the sound *seed*.

Of these eleven, one ends in *-sede*, three in *-ceed*, and the rest in *-cede*.

It may seem confusing, but it needn't be. In a minute or less, you can get these eleven demons permanently straightened out in your mind. Consider:

The *only* English word that ends in the letters S-E-D-E is *supersede*.

The *only* three words that end in C-E-E-D are *succeed*, *proceed*, and *exceed*.

*All of the other words end in C-E-D-E.*

Now let us use a couple of mnemonics.

For *supersede*, think of *Super Suds*, a famous household soap powder in its day.

For *succeed*, *proceed*, and *exceed*, remember this slogan: The driver who *succeeds* in living longer is the one who *proceeds* with caution and never *exceeds* the *speed* limit. Like *speed*, these three words in *-eed*.

Let's go over that again.

*Super* Suds—*supersede*.

*Speed*—*succeed*, *proceed*, and *exceed*.

Now begin training your visual and muscular memory. Look at each word below for a few seconds, then cover it with your hand or a slip of paper and *write* it correctly in the blank to its right.

super*sede*_____    pro*ceed*_____
suc*ceed*_____    ex*ceed*_____

More training: Write the word or words that each mnemonic brings to mind:

Super Suds:  (1)_____
Speed:  (1)_____
        (2)_____
        (3)_____

And that's all there is to it. Except for one little contradiction (and contradictions are the most normal thing in English spelling): although the C of *proceed* is followed by two E's, the noun and adjective forms have only one E after the C: procedure, procedural.

What about the other seven words? These need not be memorized, for you know that every word except *supersede, succeed, proceed,* and *exceed* ends in *-cede.* In case you are curious, however, these seven are: ac*cede,* ante*cede,* con*cede,* inter*cede,* pre*cede,* re*cede,* and se*cede.*

## TWO OTHER CONFUSING ENDINGS

Is it insist*ent* or insist*ant*? Persist*ent* or persist*ant*? Depend*ent* or depend*ant*? And how about occurr*ence* or occurr*ance,* persever*ence* or persever*ance,* abhorr*ence* or abhorr*ance*? These are confusing, pestiferous questions, yet you may have to come up with the correct answers a score of times in a busy week of writing or typing.

There are hundreds of common words ending in the alternative possibilities we are discussing, but only a relative few are frequently, almost universally, misspelled.

These are the words we shall concentrate on.

Let us conquer some of these demons by means of mnemonics.

Consider, first, the superintend*ent* of an apartm*ent* house. What does he come around to collect at the beginning of every month? The r*ent,* of course. And is he insist*ent* and persist*ent* in his collections? He is—because his job is depend*ent* on r*ent* payments. Notice, then, that the single mnemonic *rent* (which ends in *-ent*) controls four of the top demons in our language: superintend*ent,* insist*ent,* persist*ent,* and depend*ent.*

Train your visual and muscular responses to these adjectives and to the nouns derived from them. Look at each word, then conceal it with your hand or a card and write it correctly.

| | |
|---|---|
| superintend*ent*_____ | superintend*ence*_____ |
| insist*ent*_____ | insist*ence*_____ |

persist*ent*_____ persist*ence*_____
depend*ent*_____ depend*ence*_____

Now consider 11 verbs that end in the letter R:

| | |
|---|---|
| 1. in-FER | 6. oc-CUR |
| 2. pre-FER | 7. in-CUR |
| 3. re-FER | 8. con-CUR |
| 4. con-FER | 9. re-CUR |
| 5. de-FER | 10. de-TER |
| | 11. ab-HOR |

You realize that each verb is accented on the last syllable. You will notice also that in each instance the R is preceded by a *single* vowel. Now here is one of the very, very few rules of English spelling to which there is no exception: *Every verb ending in R preceded by a single vowel and accented on the final syllable forms its noun with -ence.* (Take a few seconds to memorize this principle; you will often find it a life saver.)

But wait! Do we double the R before adding *-ence*, or do we leave it alone?

We do both (nothing about spelling is easy, as you know), depending on whether the accent stays on the same syllable when the noun is formed or whether it shifts back to the first syllable.

Look at the last six verbs in the list. In each case, the accent remains on the same syllable when we add *-ence:* oc-CUR and oc-CUR-rence, in-CUR and in-CUR-rence, etc. When the accent stays put, we double the R.

Practice on these:

occu*rrence*_____ recu*rrence*_____
incu*rrence*_____ dete*rrence*_____
concu*rrence*_____ abho*rrence*_____

Now, on the other hand, see what happens with the

first five verbs. In each of these, the accent shifts back to the first syllable when you add -*ence:* in-FER, but IN-fer-ence; pre-FER, but PREF-er-ence; etc. When the accent shifts back, we *do not* double the R.

Practice as before:

inference_____        conference_____
preference_____       deference_____
reference_____

We have covered all except one of the words in this category that are most subject to error. This one, which for some unknown reason looks more appealing to the untrained speller when it ends in -*ence,* is correct only with the -*ance* ending: *perseverance.*

Have you got it all straight now? Study this section once again, paying particular attention to the rules and the mnemonics; then ask someone to dictate the words to you in random order. If your learning has been successful, you should make a perfect score on demons that almost everyone else finds troublesome.

# *Sixteenth Day*

## MORE MEMORY TRICKS TO MAKE YOU A PERFECT SPELLER

---

By now you should be convinced that *mnemonics* make mastery of correct spelling practically effortless. Today you conquer once and for all time 23 new words that are frequently misspelled.

---

### *ANOTHER CONFUSING ENDING*

You think *-ance, -ence* is hard? There is an ending that is far worse, far more confusing, far more contradictory.

Which, for example, is correct: depend*able*, or depend*ible*? irrit*able* or irrit*ible*? indispens*able* or indispens*ible*? irresist*able* or irresist*ible*? inimit*able* or inimit*ible*?

Here again, as in the previous section, we are fortunate: only five words with this confounding ending are generally misspelled. There is no reliable rule to keep you straight; there is no rhyme or reason that governs the correct choice. Each of the five demons has to be learned by itself *but can be remembered quite easily by means of mnemonics.*

For example:

| CORRECT SPELLING | MNEMONIC |
|---|---|
| 1. depend*able* | An *able* man is both depend*able* and |
| 2. indispens*able* | indispens*able*. |
| 3. irresist*ible* | Women use l*i*pst*i*ck to look irresist*i*ble (the only vowel in *lipstick* is *i*). |
| 4. irrit*able* | The verb is irrit*ate*. |
| 5. inimit*able* | The verb is imit*ate*. |

Easy? Nothing to it. Study these mnemonics once again: then write the word that fits each definition:

1. unable to be imitated_____
2. able to be depended on_____
3. able to be irritated; grumpy_____
4. unable to be resisted_____
5. absolutely essential; cannot be dispensed with_____

## AND STILL MORE ENDINGS

The next problem is: When does a verb end in *-ify* and when does it end in *-efy*?

And the answer is: Every common English verb which allows of such a choice ends in *-ify* *except four archdemons that even the most educated writers are likely to come a cropper on.*

The four archdemons: liqu*efy*, rar*efy*, stup*efy*, and putr*efy*.

Rarely, if ever, will you find a person who spells these words correctly, or even *doubts* that he is spelling them correctly when he *misspells* them. (Try your friends on the four words; stubborn souls will bet money that the *incorrect* form is *correct!*)

So practice on, and remember, these four exceptions:

1. liqu*efy*_____  3. stup*efy*_____
2. rar*efy*_____  4. putr*efy*_____

And end every other word with *-ify: classify. testify, clarify, edify, mortify,* etc.

Of course, derived forms of the four verbs also use an E where you might expect an I: liqu*e*fied, liqu*e*faction; rar*e*fied, rar*e*faction; stup*e*fied, stup*e*faction; putr*e*fied, putr*e*faction; etc.

## SPECIAL MEMORY-ASSOCIATION TRICKS

The ability to spell correctly is dependent on *memory, habit,* and *educated vision.* First, you must *remember* the precise combination of letters that make up a word. Then you must use that combination so often that it becomes an *automatic process,* requiring no thought, no figuring out. And finally, every other combination, no matter how close or similar, must *look* utterly wrong.

Apply these three cardinal principles in mastering the following 29 frequently misspelled words. *Examine* each demon carefully, focusing your attention on the italicized letters that highlight the areas where most people fall into error. *Study the mnemonic* that will fix the correct pattern in your memory. *Look* at the complete word again. Then conceal the spelling and write the word on a sheet of paper, so that you begin to develop the habit of using only the correct pattern.

1. *all* right: Always two words, no matter what the meaning. Think of the opposite, *all* wrong.

2. *in*oculate: Think of its synonym *in*ject, which also has only *one* N, *one* C.

3. ba*tt*a*l*ion: A ba*tt*a*l*ion engages in ba*ttle*—*two* T's, *one* L.

4. fri*c*a*ss*ee: May be cooked in a *c*a*ss*erole—*one* C, *two* S's.

5. anoint: We anoint with an oil; one N only before the O.

6. embarrassed: *Two* robbers were embarrassed in Sing Sing—*two* R's (two robbers), *two* S's (Sing Sing).

7. repetition: Think of repeat—E (not I) follows the P.

8. recommend: This is the verb *commend* plus the prefix *re-*; hence *one* C, *two* M's.

9. drunkenness: The adjective *drunken* (as in a *drunken bum*) plus the usual noun ending, *-ness*; hence *two* N's where most people incorrectly use only one.

10. tyranny: Think of the phrase "Down with tyrants!" which has *one* R, *two* N's.

11. category: The synonym *section* will remind you to use E where the untrained speller by error writes A.

12. occasional: *One* S, not two, by analogy with *treasure, measure, pleasure,* etc., all of which have the same sound for the single S.

13. and 14. separate, comparative: Look for *a rat* in both, thus avoiding the common incorrect forms *seperate* and *comparitive*.

Let us stop halfway for study and practice. Here are the first 14 words correctly spelled, with the troublesome areas highlighted. *Look* at them, once again, thus educating your *vision; recall* the mnemonic for each (all right—*all wrong,* inoculate—*inject,* etc.), thus educating your *memory*; and then *write* the word correctly in the blank to the right, thus educating your *muscles.*

1. all right_____    8. recommend_____
2. inoculate_____    9. drunkenness_____
3. battalion_____   10. tyranny_____
4. fricassee_____   11. category_____
5. anoint_____      12. occasional_____
6. embarrassed_____ 13. separate_____
7. repetition_____  14. comparative_____

# *Seventeenth Day*

## AND STILL MORE TRICKS

---

Another 15 words you can conquer through *mnemonics*.

---

### *MORE MNEMONICS*

And now we turn to the last 15 demons that can be best and most quickly conquered by means of mnemonics.

15. *iridescent:* This word, meaning displaying colors like a rainbow, should remind you of the *iris*, the colored portion of the eye. Both *iris* and *rainbow* have only *one* R.

16. *vilify:* This verb means to call someone *vile*; hence *one* L.

17. *disappoint:* A*pp*oint plus the prefix *dis-*; hence *one* S, *two* P's.

18. *disappear:* As above, a*pp*ear plus *dis-;* hence again *one* S, *two* P's.

19. *dissipate:* But this word is entirely different and can be remembered by analogy with the previous two words precisely because it *is* different. *Two* S's, *one* P, with an I in between.

20. *ecstasy:* *Sy* (sigh) with ecstasy, an atrocious pun

but a wonderfully helpful mnemonic to remind you that the correct ending is *-sy*, not *-cy*.

21. exhi*la*rated: If you feel exhi*la*rated, you're often hi*la*rious; both words come from the same root and both have LA after the HI.

22. coo*ll*y: Just add the adverbial ending *-ly* to *cool*, hence *two* L's.

23. *vic*ious: Think of the allied word *vice* and you will be able to resist the temptation to misspell it *viscious*.

24. *ball*oon: This is usually round, like a *ball*; hence *two* L'S.

25. va*c*uum: Means emptiness, or va*c*ant space; like vacant, *one* C only.

26. sacri*le*gious: This word is *opposite*, in a sense, to re*li*gious; hence the E and I are in *opposite* order. Do not write *sacreligious*.

27. gram*mar*: Don't let poor gram*mar mar* your speech.

28. defin*i*tely: Think of defin*i*tion; hence I, not A, follows the N.

29. descend*a*nt: Every descend*a*nt has an *a*ncestor; hence *-ant*, not *-ent*.

Practice as before:

| | |
|---|---|
| 15. iride*sc*ent_____ | 23. *vic*ious_____ |
| 16. vi*l*ify_____ | 24. *ball*oon_____ |
| 17. disa*pp*oint_____ | 25. va*c*uum_____ |
| 18. disa*pp*ear_____ | 26. sacri*le*gious_____ |
| 19. dis*si*pate_____ | 27. gram*mar*_____ |
| 20. ecsta*sy*_____ | 28. defin*i*tely_____ |
| 21. exhi*la*rated_____ | 29. descend*a*nt_____ |
| 22. coo*ll*y_____ | |

By now you should have full control over these 29 confusing words and should have no difficulty when you meet some of them in the test on a later page.

## LET'S UNCONFUSE THESE CONFUSING PAIRS

*Stationary* and *stationery* are pronounced identically; so are *principal* and *principle*. How do you know which spelling to use when?

Mnemonics will again come to your rescue.

Station*er*y consists of pap*er* and other things for writing; the ER of pap*er* tells you to spell it station*er*y. Station*a*ry, on the other hand, means st*a*nding in one pl*a*ce; the A of st*a*nding and pl*a*ce tells you to spell it station*a*ry.

A principle is a ru*le*; hence -LE at the end. We try to live by ethical *principles*, we follow certain spelling *principles*, etc. Princip*a*l, on the other hand, is either an adjective meaning m*a*in or a noun meaning m*a*in person thing, or amount; and the A of m*a*in reminds you to use -AL. For example, New York is the *principal* (main) seaport of the east coast; the *principal* of a school is the *main* teacher; the *principals* of a play are the *main* actors; and your *principal* in the bank is the *main* amount on which interest is paid.

Now do you have those four words properly unconfused? Then check the correct form in each sentence.

1. His (principal, principle) business is selling shoes.
2. The (principal, principle) of the school banks his money where 8¼% is paid on the (principal, principle).
3. He is having new (stationary, stationery) printed.
4. A (stationary, stationery) object does not move.
5. He is a man of (principal, principle).

KEY: 1—principal, 2—principal, principal, 3—stationery, 4—stationary, 5—principle.

## WHERE TO DOT YOUR I'S

To learn, once and for all, when to write *ie* and when to write *ei* is relatively simple. It is based on the following rhyme, which you probably learned in school:

I before *E*
Except after *C*
Or when sounded like *A*
As in *neighbor* or *weigh*.

Thus we use *-ei* in words like the following, because the *immediately preceding* letter is *C:* rece*i*ve, rece*i*pt, ce*i*ling, conce*i*ve, conce*i*t, dece*i*ve, etc.

But we write *-ie* in words like the following, where the immediately preceding letter is *not C:* bel*ie*ve, n*ie*ce, s*ie*ge, f*ie*ld, ach*ie*ve, p*ie*ce, br*ie*f, etc.

What, no exceptions? But of course—and the exceptions are the words that cause the most grief. Study, and practice, the following:

1. *seize*＿＿＿＿＿＿＿＿＿
2. *seizure*＿＿＿＿＿＿＿
3. *leisure*＿＿＿＿＿＿＿＿
4. *weird*＿＿＿＿＿＿＿＿＿
5. *sheik*＿＿＿＿＿＿＿＿＿
6. *financier*＿＿＿＿＿＿

(*Either* and *neither* also violate the rule, as do *ancient* and *conscience,* but few people misspell them.)

Keep these six words in mind, become accustomed to their appearance, and you'll have no trouble deciding where to put the *E*'s and *I*'s.

## ONE LAST WORD

Let's wind up with a word that even the most sophisticated speller is likely to misspell. That word is the name for the small Hawaiian guitar—the one

beginning with *uk* . . . How would you spell it? Write it in the following blank before we go on:_____
Ten to one you wrote *ukelele*. Now ask some of your friends. You may get all sorts of weird combinations, but *ukelele* is the *incorrect* pattern most frequently found.

What is correct? Believe it or not, UK*U*LELE! Watch that second *U*—no other spelling is acceptable.

## A FINAL TEST OF YOUR LEARNING

Now we are ready to make a new test of your ability as a speller. A random selection of 34 of the special demons we have discussed appears below—some correctly spelled, some as they are usually misspelled. Your job is to decide, without hesitation or confusion, which is which. If a word is correct, check the space next to it; if it is incorrect, rewrite it correctly.

| | |
|---|---|
| 1. irridescent_____ | 18. achieve_____ |
| 2. inimitible_____ | 19. drunkeness_____ |
| 3. putrify_____ | 20. dissapoint_____ |
| 4. superintendant_____ | 21. supercede_____ |
| 5. tyranny_____ | 22. ukelele_____ |
| 6. ecstacy_____ | 23. coolly_____ |
| 7. indispensable_____ | 24. irresistable_____ |
| 8. dependant_____ | 25. disappate_____ |
| 9. descendant_____ | 26. occurence_____ |
| 10. vilify_____ | 27. seperate_____ |
| 11. proceed_____ | 28. seize_____ |
| 12. sacreligious_____ | 29. alright_____ |
| 13. inoculate_____ | 30. definately_____ |
| 14. embarrassed_____ | 31. neice_____ |
| 15. anoint_____ | 32. wierd_____ |
| 16. occassional_____ | 33. liquefy_____ |
| 17. perseverance_____ | 34. recieve_____ |

KEY: 1—iridescent, 2—inimitable, 3—putrefy, 4—superintendent, 5—√, 6—ecstasy, 7—√, 8—dependent, 9—√, 10—√
11—√, 12—sacrilegious, 13—√, 14—√, 15—√, 16—occasional
17—√, 18—√, 19—drunkenness, 20—disappoint, 21—supersede, 22—ukulele, 23—√, 24—irresistible, 25—dissipate,
26—occurrence, 27—separate, 28—√, 29—all right, 30—
definitely, 31—niece, 32—weird, 33—√, 34—receive.

# *Eighteenth Day*

## SOME MORE SPELLING TESTS TO KEEP YOU ALERT

By now you should really *feel* your spelling ability improving—but don't relax. The next five tests will check on your learning and introduce some new demons for you to conquer.

### Test 1

This is a most devilish and inconsiderate way to test your spelling powers. Probably if you were asked right out to spell any of the 15 words below you could do so without error. But really to test your ability, the words are distributed in groups of three, and in each group only *one* word is *misspelled*. Find that one in three groups and your ability is average; find all five and you have something to be proud of.

1. (a) disippate (b) absence (c) assassin
2. (a) assistant (b) ukulele (c) truely
3. (a) coolly (b) newstand (c) drunkenness
4. (a) suppress (b) dumfound (c) baloon
5. (a) benifit (b) connoisseur (c) ecstasy

## Test 2

Of the following 20 words, exactly 10 are misspelled. It is up to you to identify and rewrite the improper forms.

|   |   |   |   |
|---|---|---|---|
| 1. | unpredictible | 11. | attendance |
| 2. | developement | 12. | cargoes |
| 3. | yield | 13. | reccomend |
| 4. | occassion | 14. | feminine |
| 5. | privilege | 15. | dependible |
| 6. | committee | 16. | resistent |
| 7. | embarassed | 17. | hazzard |
| 8. | superintendant | 18. | raccoon |
| 9. | announce | 19. | professor |
| 10. | desparately | 20. | gaiety |

## Test 3

Oddly enough, it's not the obscure word that causes the most trouble, but the common, everyday word, the word that looks reasonable and correct no matter in which of two popular ways you write it.

Here is a test which will check your familiarity with the correct forms of commonly misspelled words. Two patterns are offered, and it is up to you to check the one proper form. Fourteen to 15 right is **remarkable**, 11 to 13 good, 9 or 10 average.

1. (a) existence (b) existance
2. (a) beginning (b) begining
3. (a) foriegn (b) foreign
4. (a) buisness (b) business
5. (a) conceivable (b) concievable
6. (a) ukulele (b) ukelele
7. (a) holliday (b) holiday
8. (a) differant (b) different

 9. (a) phenomenal (b) phenominal
10. (a) aggreed (b) agreed
11. (a) liesurely (b) leisurely
12. (a) dissapear (b) disappear
13. (a) labeled (b) labled
14. (a) benificial (b) beneficial
15. (a) femenine (b) feminine

## Test 4

In each line are three words, one of them purposely misspelled. It's up to you to check and respell correctly the one error on each line. Six right is average, 7 to 8 good, 9 to 10 superior.

 1. all right, recommend, innoculate
 2. holiday, arguement, absence
 3. drunkeness, coolly, grammar
 4. supercede, definitely, repetition
 5. dissipate, pronounciation, superintendent
 6. irresistable, insistent, category
 7. license, exhilarate, embarassing
 8. ecstacy, benefited, whisky
 9. genealogy, picnicer, sergeant
10. developement, elopement, receive

## Test 5

Here are 20 real demons—half spelled correctly and half spelled as many of us think they're spelled. Can you check the 10 that are *correct*?

 1. peaceable
 2. irritible
 3. defense
 4. surprise
 5. sherrif
 6. grammar
 7. preceed
 8. accoustics
 9. kidnaped
10. concientious

11. insistant
12. developement
13. vicious
14. supersede
15. whisky

16. repitition
17. suddeness
18. likable
19. trafficking
20. definately

KEY

1: 1–a (*dissipate*), 2–c (*truly*), 3–b (*newsstand*), 4–c (*balloon*), 5–a (*benefit*).

2: Correct spellings: 1–unpredictable, 2–development, 4–occasion, 7–embarrassed, 8–superintendent, 10–desperately, 13–recommend. 15–dependable, 16–resistant, 17–hazard.

3: 1–a, 2–a, 3–b, 4–b, 5–a, 6–a, 7–b, 8–b, 9–a, 10–b, 11–b, 12–b, 13–a, 14–b, 15–b.

4: 1–*innoculate* should be *inoculate*, 2–*arguement* should be *argument*, 3–*drunkeness* should be *drunkenness*, 4–*supercede* should be *supersede*, 5–*pronounciation* should be *pronunciation*, 6–*irresistable* should be *irresistible*, 7–*embarassing* should be *embarrassing*, 8–*ecstacy* should be *ecstasy*, 9–*picnicer* should be *picnicker*, 10–*developement* should be *development*.

5: Correct forms are 1, 3, 4, 6, 9, 13, 14, 15, 18, 19. Incorrect forms are spelled as follows:

2–irritable
5–sheriff
7–precede
8–acoustics
10–conscientious

11–insistent
12–development
16–repetition
17–suddenness
20–definitely

# Nineteenth Day

## A FINAL, ACID TEST OF YOUR NEWLY ACQUIRED SPELLING SKILL

Some of the hundred words tested in this chapter you've already conquered—others are new. When you've mastered the new ones, you'll be sure of one thing—it will be a cold day in August before anyone can ever stump you again!

*Part I: Elementary.* Get all 25 right to consider that your spelling contains no hint of illiteracy. Check the correct form in each case.

1. (a) too, (b) to (He is getting_____fat.)
2. (a) it's, (b) its (It spent_____power.)
3. (a) their, (b) there (They took off_____coats.)
4. (a) grammer, (b) grammar
5. (a) amoung, (b) among
6. (a) receive, (b) recieve
7. (a) therefore, (b) therefor (meaning *consequently*)
8. (a) immediately, (b) immediatly
9. (a) buisness, (b) business
10. (a) seperate, (b) separate
11. (a) benefit, (b) benifit
12. (a) lose, (b) loose (We will_____money.)
13. (a) untill, (b) until

14. (a) doesn't, (b) dosen't
15. (a) coming, (b) comming
16. (a) ocurred, (b) occurred
17. (a) neccessary, (b) necessary
18. (a) existence, (b) existance
19. (a) appeerence, (b) appearance
20. (a) accross, (b) across
21. (a) discription, (b) description
22. (a) your, (b) you're (Is that what_____doing?)
23. (a) supprise, (b) surprise
24. (a) weird, (b) wierd
25. (a) friend, (b) freind

*Part II: Intermediate.* Get at least 21 right to feel that your spelling is better than average; 17 right to grade it average. Check the correct form in each case.

1. (a) occassion, (b) occasion
2. (a) villain, (b) villian
3. (a) acommodate, (b) accommodate
4. (a) occurrence, (b) occurrance
5. (a) truely, (b) truly
6. (a) fourty, (b) forty
7. (a) pursue, (b) persue
8. (a) arguement, (b) argument
9. (a) dissappear, (b) disappear
10. (a) dissappoint, (b) disappoint
11. (a) neice, (b) niece
12. (a) privilege, (b) priviledge
13. (a) alright, (b) all right
14. (a) desireable, (b) desirable
15. (a) addresses, (b) addreses
16. (a) dispair, (b) despair
17. (a) definitely, (b) definately
18. (a) developement, (b) development
19. (a) irresistible, (b) irresistable
20. (a) sargeant, (b) sergeant

21. (a) noticable, (b) noticeable
22. (a) lonelyness, (b) loneliness
23. (a) vengance, (b) vengeance
24. (a) procede, (b) proceed
25. (a) conscientious, (b) concientious

*Part III: Advanced.* Get 20 or more right and you may confidently boast that your spelling is downright good; get all 25 right to label your ability excellent. Check the correct form in each case.

1. (a) batallion, (b) battalion
2. (a) disasterous, (b) disastrous
3. (a) embarassing, (b) embarrassing
4. (a) benefited, (b) benefitted
5. (a) balloon, (b) baloon
6. (a) rythmical, (b) rhythmical
7. (a) indispensible, (b) indispensable
8. (a) sacrilegious, (b) sacreligious
9. (a) superintendant, (b) superintendent
10. (a) passtime, (b) pastime
11. (a) parallel, (b) paralell
12. (a) exhilaration, (b) exhillaration
13. (a) irrelevant, (b) irrelevent
14. (a) tyrranize, (b) tyrannize
15. (a) repetition, (b) repitition
16. (a) perseverance, (b) perseverence
17. (a) grievious, (b) grievous
18. (a) irritible, (b) irritable
19. (a) reccomend, (b) recommend
20. (a) rediculous, (b) ridiculous
21. (a) acceed, (b) accede
22. (a) cooly, (b) coolly
23. (a) supercede, (b) supersede
24. (a) absence, (b) abscence
25. (a) anoint, (b) annoint

*Part IV: Postgraduate.* Get all 25 right and you are undoubtedly a perfect speller; or get at least 20 right to claim that you are practically perfect. Check the correct form in each case.

1. (a) eliptical, (b) elliptical
2. (a) dissipation, (b) disippation
3. (a) ecstasy, (b) ecstacy
4. (a) ukulele, (b) ukelele
5. (a) khaki, (b)kahki
6. (a) innoculate, (b) inoculate
7. (a) drunkeness, (b) drunkenness
8. (a) insistant, (b) insistent
9. (a) persistant, (b) persistent
10. (a) corroborate, (b) corobborate
11. (a) vaccilate, (b) vacillate
12. (a) dilletante, (b) dilettante
13. (a) panicy, (b) panicky
14. (a) vaccuum, (b) vacuum
15. (a) plebian, (b) plebeian
16. (a) tariff, (b) tarrif
17. (a) sheriff, (b) sherrif
18. (a) connoisseur, (b) conoisseur
19. (a) naïveté, (b) naivety
20. (a) accelerator, (b) accelerater
21. (a) broccoli, (b) brocolli
22. (a) racoon, (b) raccoon
23. (a) catarrh, (b) cattarrh
24. (a) pleurisy, (b) pleurasy
25. (a) irridescent, (b) iridescent

KEY

*Part I:* 1–a, 2–b, 3–a, 4–b, 5–b, 6–a, 7–a, 8–a, 9–b, 10–b, 11–a, 12–a, 13–b, 14–a, 15–a, 16–b, 17–b, 18–a, 19–b, 20–b, 21–b, 22–b, 23–b, 24–a, 25–a.

*Part II:* 1–b, 2–a, 3–b, 4–a, 5–b, 6–b, 7–a, 8–b, 9–b, 10–b, 11–b, 12–a, 13–b, 14–b, 15–a, 16–b, 17–a, 18–b, 19–a, 20–b, 21–b, 22–b, 23–b, 24–b, 25–a.

*Part III:* 1–b, 2–b, 3–b, 4–a, 5–a, 6–b, 7–b, 8–a, 9–b, 10–b, 11–a, 12–a, 13–a, 14–b, 15–a, 16–a, 17–b, 18–b, 19–b, 20–b, 21–b, 22–b, 23–b, 24–a, 25–a.

*Part IV:* 1–b, 2–a, 3–a, 4–a, 5–a, 6–b, 7–b, 8–b, 9–b, 10–a, 11–b, 12–b, 13–b, 14–b, 15–b, 16–a, 17–a, 18–a, 19–a, 20–a, 21–a, 22–b, 23–a, 24–a, 25–b.

# *Twentieth Day*

## JUST FOR FUN (IV)

### *DO WORDS CONFUSE YOU?*

One of the basic steps that a person often takes in learning a new word involves a normal sense of confusion between its actual meaning and its opposite meaning. Below you will find 15 important and valuable words, each followed by a phrase which is either essentially the *same* or more nearly *opposite* in meaning to the key word. It's up to you to decide which is which. Par on this test is 9 correct decisions. How well can you do?

1. enervated —exhausted; worn out S ( ) O ( )
2. sacrilegious —excessively pious or S ( ) O ( )
   God-fearing
3. abject —full of haughtiness S ( ) O ( )
4. adulation —overabundant S ( ) O ( )
   flattery
5. dearth —great deficiency S ( ) O ( )
6. carnivorous —avoiding meat S ( ) O ( )
7. convivial —grumpy and S ( ) O ( )
   unsociable
8. insidious —working secretly S ( ) O ( )
   or subtly
9. expiate —atone for S ( ) O ( )

10. frugality    \_\_unnecessary     S (    O ·
                 extravagance

11. indolent     \_\_full of ambition    S ( ) O ·
                 and energy

12. senile       \_\_mentally and      S ( ) O ( )
                 physically weak
                 from advanced age

13. verbose     \_\_unusually quiet;    S ( ) O ( ·
                 using few words

14. parsimonious \_\_miserly, overly    S ( ) O ( ·
                 economical

15. suave        \_\_smoothly agreeable S ( ) O ( ·
                 or polite

KEY:   1—same, 2—opposite, 3—opposite, 4—same, 5— same, 6—opposite, 7—opposite, 8—same, 9—same, 10—opposite, 11—opposite, 12—same, 13—opposite, 14—same, 15—same.

## *HOW IS YOUR PRONUNCIATION?*

When you use a word, do you generally pronounce it according to educated standards? Test yourself by checking what you consider the correct pronunciation of each of the 15 words below.

1. canapé (an appetizer): (a) kə-NAYP', (b) ka-na-PAY'
2. asphalt (a kind of paving): (a) ASS'-fawlt, (b) ASH'-fawlt
3. zoology (the science of animals): (a) zō-OL'-ə-jee, (b) zoo-OL'-ə-jee
4. respite (a pause): (a) RES'-pit, (b) rə-SPITE'
5. thyme (a flavoring): (a) TIME, (b) THIME
6. efficacy (effectiveness): (a) ə-FICK'-ə-see, (b) EFF'-ə-kə-see

7. regime (a system): (a) rə-ZHEEM′ (ZH is the sound of S in *pleasure*), (b) rə-JEEM′
8. scourge (an affliction): (a) SKURJ, (b) SKORJ
9. sachet (a scent bag): (a) SASH′-et, (b) sa-SHAY′
10. indefatigable (tireless): (a) in-də-FAT′-ə-gə-bəl, (b) in-də-fə-TEEG′-ə-bəl
11. trespasser (encroacher): (a) tress-PASS′-ər, (b) TRESS′-pə-sər
12. viscount (a nobleman); (a) VYE′-kount, (b) VIS′-kount
13. alias (an assumed name): (a) ə-LYE′-əs, (b) AY′-lee-əs
14. chameleon (an animal): (a) CHAM′-ə-lon, (b) kə-MEE′-lee-ən
15. clandestine (secret): (a) klan-DES′-tin, (b) CLAN′-də-styne

KEY: 1–b, 2–a, 3–a, 4–a, 5–a, 6–b, 7–a, 8–a, 9–b, 10–a, 11–b, 12–a, 13–b, 14–b, 15–a.

## *AROUND THE ALPHABET—AND BACK AGAIN*

If a word is offered to you, can you immediately respond with an antonym?

This exercise is an acid test of the speed and accuracy of your verbal reactions. For each key word below, write another, of essentially *opposite* meaning, which begins with the indicated letter. *Allow yourself ten minutes— not a second more.* Par for the course is 30; expert rating is 40. How well can *you* do?

1. purposely    a_____
2. harmful      b_____
3. expensive    c_____
4. wet          d_____
5. calm         e_____

6. to sink          f_____
7. harsh            g_____
8. low              h_____
9. genius           i_____
10. solemn          j_____
11. to relinquish   k_____
12. careful         l_____
13. phobia          m_____
14. synthetic       n_____
15. transparent     o_____
16. reward          p_____
17. agreement       q_____
18. slow            r_____
19. land            s_____
20. permanent       t_____
21. above           u_____
22. occupied        v_____
23. ruddy           w_____
24. today           y_____
25. straight        z_____
26. indifferent     z_____
27. white of egg    y_____
28. strong          w_____
29. silent          v_____
30. commonplace     u_____
31. practice        t_____
32. frivolous       s_____
33. conformist      r_____
34. answer          q_____
35. intersecting    p_____
36. young           o_____
37. both            n_____
38. magnify         m_____
39. infinite        l_____
40. dull            k_____
41. safety          j_____
42. soiled          i_____

43. sickness      h_____
44. disperse      g_____
45. mute          f_____
46. altruist      e_____
47. sure          d_____
48. unusual       c_____
49. long          b_____
50. enemy         a_____

KEY: 1—accidentally; 2—beneficial; 3—cheap, complimentary; 4—dry, desiccated; 5—excited, excitable, emotional, effervescent, ebullient; 6—float; 7—gentle, genial, gracious; 8—high, hilly; 9—idiot, imbecile; 10—jolly, jesting, jocose, jocund, joking, joyful, joyous, jovial; 11—keep; 12—lax, loose; 13—mania; 14—natural; 15—opaque, obscure; 16—punish, punishment, penalty, penalize, penance; 17—quarrel; 18—rapid; 19—sea; 20—temporary; 21—under, underneath; 22—vacant; 23—wan, waxy; 24—yesterday, yore; 25—zigzag; 26—zealous; 27—yolk; 28—weak, wasted, withered, worn; 29—verbose, voluble, vociferous; 30—unusual, uncommon, unique, unprecedented; 31—theory; 32—serious, sincere, sedate, solemn, staid; 33—rebel, revolutionary, resister; 34—question, query, quiz; 35—parallel; 36—old, obsolete; 37—neither, none; 38—minimize; 39—limited; 40—keen, knifelike; 41—jeopardy; 42—immaculate; 43—health, haleness, hardiness; 44—gather; 45—fluent, forensic; 46—egoist, egotist, egocentric, egomaniac; 47—doubtful, dubious, debatable, disbelieving, distrustful; 48—common, commonplace, conventional, customary, current; 49—brief; 50—ally.

# PART V

## *Speak Correctly!*

Correct usage, no matter how you slice it, is what educated people say and write. Those rules of English grammar that are unself-consciously observed by effective speakers, by those who have the public ear, and by professional and established authors are the ones that are important.

In Part V you will consider and thoroughly drill on three categories of these important rules—categories that account for 75 percent of the errors made by unsophisticated speakers.

# *Twenty-first Day*

## AN ENGLISH TEST FOR YOU

---

Let's find out if your everyday English is as good as you are.

---

### *ARE YOU BETTER THAN YOUR ENGLISH SAYS YOU ARE?*

When you speak to other people in your office or on your job . . .

When you get up to address a group . . .

Or when you write a letter or report that will be read by people whose judgment of your knowledge and intelligence is important to you . . .

*At such times does your command of language do you full justice, or does it sometimes fail to help you make the kind of impression you are potentially capable of making?*

When it comes to first impressions, it seems that the old saying is frequently reversed: at the beginning, at least, words speak louder than actions. That's when the English you use can be an asset—or a stumbling block in the way of acceptance. Which is it in your case? To find out whether your English works for or against you . . .

## TAKE THIS REVEALING TEST

In each sentence, check off the word you would be most likely to use in your own speech or writing.

1. Let's just keep this a secret between you and (a—I, b—me).

2. The position will be offered to either you or (a—me, b—I).

3. We found everyone home except (a—he, b—him) and his father.

4. If I were (a—she, b—her), I wouldn't act that way.

5. I know you're taller than (a—I, b—me).

6. They can work a lot faster than (a—we, b—us).

7. Please call Mrs. Brown or (a—I, b—me) whenever you need help.

8. (a—Who, b—Whom) do you expect will be appointed chairman of the dance committee next year?

9. (a—Who, b—Whom) are you waiting for?

10. The prisoner was (a—hanged, b—hung) at dawn.

11. How did his speech (a—affect, b—effect) you?

12. It was the most beautiful (a—affect, b—effect) we had ever seen.

13. Don't sound so (a—incredulous, b—incredible); what I'm saying is absolutely true.

14. That job is very difficult; (a—beside, b—besides), I'm not really trained for it.

15. Why don't you (a—lay, b—lie) down for a nap before dinner?

16. (a—Lie, b—Lay) your hand on the radiator and see how hot it is.

17. The book reports (a—lay, b—laid) on the teacher's desk all morning.

18. Has the cat (a—laid, b—lain) here all morning?

19. (a—Has, b—Have) either of your parents come in yet?

20. Neither of your suggestions (a—is, b—are) really practical.

21. Every one of his answers (a—is, b—are) correct.

22. Either the principal or his secretary (a—are, b—is) in the office at all times.

23. The cost of loose-leaf sheets (a—are, b—is) beginning to rise again.

24. How (a—is, b—are) your mother and father feeling?

25. (a—These, b—This) phenomena (a—are, b—is) worth seeing.

KEY:   1—b, 2—a, 3—b, 4—a, 5—a, 6—a, 7—b, 8—a, 9—b, 10—a, 11—a, 12—b, 13—a, 14—b, 15—b, 16—b, 17—a, 18—b, 19—a, 20—a, 21—a, 22—b, 23—b, 24—b, 25—a, a.

SCORING: EXCELLENT, 23—25 correct; GOOD, 19—22; FAIR, 13—18; POOR, 12 or less.


## *LET'S GET DOWN TO WORK*

How did you do? Don't feel dismayed if you made an incorrect choice in a great many of the sentences. For, although the English language is full of traps for the unwary, you will be amazed at how quickly and successfully you can learn to avoid the main pitfalls and booby traps of correct usage. You can master the material in this part of the book in just a few days. But within those few days you can

—take giant strides forward in improving your English;

—discover and permanently root out most of the errors you now make;

—and gain self-assurance that will help you whenever you speak or write.

How can we expect our work to be so easy and so immediately rewarding?

*Because 75 percent or more of the common errors made in grammar occur in just three broad areas of usage:*

1. Pronouns (I, you, me, him, etc.)
2. The words *lay* and *lie*
3. Singular and plural words

In Part V, most of our attention will be devoted to these three areas. As a starting point, let us learn . . .

## ALL ABOUT PRONOUNS

*Problem 1.* Shall we keep this strictly between *you and I*—or between *you and me?*
*Solution.* Probably the most common error made by people who are not quite sure of their grammar occurs in the use of the pronoun following *between.* After this word, and also after *except* and *but* (all of which are prepositions), only object pronouns are grammatically acceptable.

**Rule 1.**

Use these object pronouns after the prepositions *between, except,* and *but:* ME, HIM, HER, US, THEM.
Read the following phrases aloud:

Between *you* and *me*     No one except *him*
Between *him* and *her*     All but *me*
Between *them* and *us*     Everyone but *her*

*Problem 2.* Do you want both Paul and *I*—or Paul and *me*—to come in early tomorrow?
*Solution.* The choice of the correct word becomes particularly confusing when we have a combination either of two pronouns or of a noun and a pronoun. Consider these sentences:

1. This is for you and (*I, me?*).
2. Are you inviting Mary and (*we, us?*) to your party?
3. That's no way to treat (*we, us?*) boys.
4. George and (*he, him?*) will come in late tomorrow.
5. Do you want (*he and I, him and me?*) to help you?

Whenever you find yourself in this kind of trouble, you can apply an easy, and foolproof, rule.

*Omit, for a moment, the additional word with which the pronoun is combined, and you will unerringly make the proper choice.*

In sentence 1, omit *you*. We would naturally say, "This is for *me*"; hence, "This is for you and *me*."

In sentence 2, omit *Mary*. We have to say, "Are you inviting *us* to your party?"; hence, "Are you inviting Mary and *us*?"

In sentence 3, omit *boys*. "That's no way to treat *us*"; hence, "*us* boys."

In sentence 4, omit *George*. "*He* will come in late tomorrow"; hence, "George and *he* will come in late tomorrow."

In sentence 5, take *one* of the pronouns at a time. "Do you want *him* to help you?" "Do you want *me* to help you?" Hence, "Do you want *him* and *me* to help you?"

## Rule 2.

To figure out the correct pronoun to use in a combination, temporarily *omit* one part of the combination.

*Problem 3.* Are you taller than *me*—or taller than *I*? And do you eat as much as *me*—or as much as *I*?

*Solution.* Tuck the words *than* and *as* away in a corner of your mind. To figure out the correct pronoun to use after *either* of these two connecting words (called *conjunctions*), just finish your sentence by adding the understood *verb*. Thus:

1. Are you taller than (me, I?) *am*? (*I*)
2. Do you eat as much as (me, I?) *do*? (*I*)
3. You can't type as fast as (she, her?) *does*. (*she*)
4. We're not as rich as (them, they?) *are*. (*they*)

**Rule 3.**

To figure out the correct pronoun to use after *than* and *as*, fill in the missing *verb*.

*Problem 4.* When someone on the phone asks for Miss Brown, and *you* are Miss Brown, what should you say— this is *she*, or this is *her*?
*Solution.* We have an example here of one of the most recurrent—and most annoying—of pronoun problems. It was *he*—or *him*? It could have been *she*—or *her*? If you were *I*—or *me*?

To solve your dilemma in these instances, you must become familiar with the important forms of the verb *to be*:

**IS, ARE, AM; WAS, WERE;
HAVE, HAS and HAD BEEN**

And then, in addition, you need only bear in mind that the following subject pronouns are correctly used after any of these forms of the verb *to be*.

**I, HE, SHE, WE, THEY**

Get used to the sound of these sentences.

1. This is *she*.
2. It was *he* who did it.
3. If you were *I*, wouldn't you act the same way?
4. It is *they* I'm referring to, not you.

**Rule 4.**

After any form of the verb *to be*, use the subject pronouns *I, he, she, we, they*. However, "It's *me*," though not technically correct, is usually acceptable in informal conversation.

*Problem 5. Who* are you talking to, or *whom* are you talking to? *Who* do you see, or *whom* do you see? Is this the only person *who*—or *whom*—you feel you can trust? *Solution. Who* and *whom* are treacherous and bothersome pronouns, and there's no point in pretending otherwise. But you can avoid all the confusion that these demons usually cause by applying one simple principle.

## Rule 5.

Whenever you feel any doubt about whether to use *who* or *whom*, turn the sentence around so that you can substitute *he* or *him*. If *he* fits, the correct word is *who*; if, however, *him* fits, the correct word is *whom*.

For example, in the sentences of our problem, the only sensible English, when we rearrange the word order, is as follows: You are talking to *him*, you see *him*, you feel you can trust *him*. In all three sentences then, only *whom* is the strictly correct form.

## Study These Problems

1. (*Who, Whom*) is here? *He* is here; hence, *who*.
2. (*Who, Whom*) do you know? You know *him*; hence, *whom*.
3. (*Who, Whom*) are you calling? You're calling *him*; hence, *whom*.
4. (*Who, Whom*) are you referring to? You are referring to *him*; hence, *whom*.
5. (*Who, Whom*) do you think you are? You think you are *he* (you will recall that any form of the verb *to be* takes a subject pronoun); hence, *who*.

What do you have to know in order to be able to handle pronouns with correctness and assurance? Let us take a moment to summarize.

1. After any preposition, notably *between, except,* and *but,* use object pronouns (*me, him, her, us, them*).

2. After any form of the verb *to be,* use subject pronouns (*I, he, she, we, they*).

3. In combined forms (he and I, Jane and us, etc.), omit one element of the combination to determine whether to use a subject or object pronoun.

4. After the conjunctions *than* and *as,* fill in the understood verb.

5. To straighten yourself out on *who* and *whom,* substitute *he* or *him: who* stands for *he, whom* for *him.*

Ready for a test of your skill?

## Check Your Learning

1. Let's just keep this between you and (a—me, b—I).
2. Was it (a—he, b—him) you were worried about?
3. If you were (a—me, b—I), what would you do?
4. I'm not as fast as (a—him, b—he).
5. They work a lot harder than (a—us, b—we).
6. I will call (a—he, b—him) and his wife tomorrow.
7. Was the letter addressed to you and (a—me, b—I)?
8. She is one woman (a—who, b—whom) I really admire.
9. (a—Who, b—Whom) did you come to see?
10. (a—Who, b—Whom) are you waiting for?
11. (a—Who, b—Whom) are you talking about?
12. (a—Who, b—Whom) would you like to be?

KEY:   1—a, 2—a, 3—b, 4—b, 5—b, 6—b, 7—a ,8—b, 9—b, 10—b, 11—b, 12—a.

# *Twenty-second Day*

## THE MOST CONFUSING VERBS IN THE ENGLISH LANGUAGE, AND HOW TO GET THEM STRAIGHT

---

No other verbs cause as much trouble as *lay* and *lie*. Now you can begin mastering them by learning a few simple and easy-to-apply principles.

---

### ALL ABOUT LAY AND LIE

*Problem 6.* Do you *lay* down—or *lie* down—for a nap before dinner?

*Solution.* Although *lay* and *lie* are without doubt the most confusing—and confused—pair of verbs in the English language, and although they are a source of never-ending contradiction and bewilderment to many people, you can learn how to untangle them before you come to the end of this chapter.

*Understanding* the distinction between *lay* and *lie* is child's play. *Training yourself* to observe this distinction whenever you speak will require a little more effort.

This is all you have to know:

*Lay* means to *place* or *put* something or someone somewhere.

*Lie* means to *recline, rest,* or *remain.*

Now you must admit that nothing could be simpler or more clear-cut than that.

You *lay* (*place*) a book on the table; you *lay* (*place*) a child in its crib; you *lay* (*put*) in a supply of coal.

You *lie* (*remain*) asleep; the penny was *lying* (*resting*) in the mud; you *lie* down (*recline*) for a nap.

Clear so far? But wait, it gets just a bit more complicated in the past and perfect tenses.

Today you *lie* down for a nap; yesterday you *lay* down for a nap (*past tense*); you *have lain* asleep all morning (*perfect tense*—the form used with *has, have,* or *had.*)

It is in the past and perfect tenses that most of the errors are made, so study the previous paragraph until you understand it thoroughly.

And commit this simple chart to memory:

### To Recline, etc.
### LIE, LAY, HAVE LAIN

The past and perfect tenses of *lay, to place,* offer no difficulty. Today you *lay* the book on the table; yesterday you *laid* it on the table (*past tense*); you *have laid* the book on the table (*perfect tense*).

Here is a final chart to memorize, and then you know everything there is to know about *lay* and *lie.*

### To Place, etc.
### LAY, LAID, HAVE LAID

Now read the following sentences aloud, get used to their sound, and understand precisely why each form is used.

### *LIE*

1. *Lie* down, please. (recline)
2. The dog was *lying* on the sofa. (reclining)
3. Did you *lie* down for a nap after dinner? (recline)
4. He *lay* quietly while the doctor examined him. (reclined, past tense)
5. The report *has lain* on the president's desk all week. (remained, perfect tense)

### *LAY*

1. *Lay* your hands on mine. (place)
2. *Lay* the child on its back. (place)
3. He *laid* his hand on mine. (placed, past tense)
4. He *has laid* my fears to rest. (placed, perfect tense)

Let us see how skillfully you can avoid *lay-lie* traps.

## Check Your Learning

1. The dog is (a—laying, b—lying) on the sofa.
2. Why don't you (a—lie, b—lay) down for a short nap?
3. The wounded man (a—laid, b—lay) in the gutter.
4. She has (a—lain, b—laid) asleep all morning.
5. These items have (a—lain, b—laid) on the shelf all month.
6. Did you (a—lie, b—lay) on the beach last Sunday?

KEY:  1–b, 2–a, 3–b, 4–a, 5–a, 6–a.

# *Twenty-third Day*

## FINAL STEPS FOR MASTERING LAY AND LIE

---

Today you nail down your understanding of these troublesome verbs and prove to yourself that you can now avoid all confusion.

---

### *MOP-UP ON LAY AND LIE*

Easy so far? Then let's really nail the correct forms home so you'll never again be confused. *Lay*, I have said, means *put; lie* means *recline, rest,* or *remain.* The present participle of *lie* is, of course, *lying;* of *lay, laying.* Can you, then, zip through these 10 sentences, checking the correct word in each one?

1. When we (a–lie, b–lay) on the bed, we can feel the springs.
2. If you (a–lie, b–lay) away a few dollars every week, you will soon be able to buy that bicycle.
3. (a–Lay, b–Lie) still for a few minutes.
4. (Don't (a–lay, b–lie) the books on that high shelf.
5. (a–Lay, b–Lie) your composition on my desk.

6. We found the wounded man (a—laying, b—lying) on the floor.

7. He is accustomed to (a—laying, b—lying) down for a short nap after dinner.

8. (a—Lie, b—Lay) the baby in its crib.

9. We saw a penny (a—laying, b—lying) in the mud.

10. He was (a—laying, b—lying) in bed watching television.

KEY:   1—a, 2—b, 3—b, 4—a, 5—a, 6—b, 7—b, 8—b, 9—b, 10—b.


## HOW ABOUT PAST TENSES?

So now you may consider yourself an expert in the simple part of *lay* and *lie*. But how good are you in the past and perfect tenses, which are much harder? Before you do the next test, keep three points in mind:

1. The past of *lie* (to recline, etc.) is *LAY*.
   The past of *lay* (to put) is *LAID*.
   For example:
   I *lay* in bed so long this morning, I was late for school.
   I *laid* my clothes out the night before, so I was able to sleep ten minutes longer.

2. After the auxiliary verb *did*, use the present tense of *lie* (recline, etc.) and of *lay* (put, place) —*did* is a past tense marker and so the main verb should not be put in the past.
   For example:
   *Did* you *lie* down?
   No, I *did* not *lie* down.
   *Did* you *lay* your clothes away?
   No, I *did* not *lay* my clothes away.

3. The perfect tense of *lie* (recline) is *has, have,* or *had lain*.

The perfect tense of *lay* (put, place) is *has, have,* or *had laid*.

For example:

*Has* your mother *lain* down for a nap?

The baby *has lain* asleep for over three hours.

*Have* you *laid* your homework on Miss Brown's desk?

### READY FOR A TEST?

I. Check the correct form.
  1. She (lay, laid) down for a nap.
  2. When she (lay, laid) down for a nap, her dinner burned.
  3. She (lay, laid) the work aside for a few minutes.
  4. The nurse (lay, laid) the patient on his back.
  5. They (lay, laid) the foundation of the building.
  6. He (lay, laid) quietly for a few minutes.
  7. Did you (lay, lie) down for a nap?
  8. Did you (lay, lie) the baby down?

II. Check the correct past participle.
  1. Has he (laid, lain) here long?
  2. Have you (laid, lain) away your woolens?
  3. Had he (laid, lain) quietly, this would not have happened.
  4. After he had (laid, lain) his books down, he sat down to dinner.
  5. Has she (laid, lain) asleep all day?
  6. Where have you (laid, lain) my things?
  7. His crime has (laid, lain) on his conscience all year.
  8. The diamond has (laid, lain) on his desk for months, and no one ever noticed it.

III. Now, as a general review, check the correct verb.
  1. The patient is (lying, laying) down.
  2. (Lie, Lay) the baby down.
  3. Estelle has (laid, lain) down for a nap.

4. He picked up the sticks and (laid, lay) them straight.

5. We (laid, lay) in the sun all morning.

6. He (laid, lay) his hands on the controls and waited for the signal to start.

7. Have you (laid, lain) away your summer clothing?

8. The bill has (laid, lain) on the President's desk all week.

9. Which shelf did you (lie, lay) the curtains on?

10. The diamond (laid, lay) in the gutter all day, and no one saw it.

11. Did you (lay, lie) on your back all night?

12. Let sleeping dogs (lay, lie).

13. He was (lying, laying) on the floor.

14. Let us (lay, lie) our plans carefully.

15. All morning, he (laid, lay) in wait.

16. (Lay, Lie) down, please.

17. (Lay, Lie) your hand on mine.

18. I won't (lay, lie) down.

19. I can't stand all this junk (laying, lying) around.

20. He loves to (lay, lie) in the sun and watch the ships pass by.

KEY

I. 1–lay, 2–lay, 3–laid, 4–laid, 5–laid, 6–lay, 7–lie, 8–lay.

II. 1–lain, 2–laid, 3–lain, 4–laid, 5–lain, 6–laid, 7–lain, 8–lain.

III. 1–lying, 2–lay, 3–lain, 4–laid, 5–lay, 6–laid, 7–laid, 8–lain, 9–lay, 10–lay, 11–lie, 12–lie, 13–lying, 14–lay, 15–lay, 16–lie, 17–lay, 18–lie, 19–lying, 20–lie.

# *Twenty-fourth Day*

## HOW TO FIND YOUR WAY THROUGH SINGULARS AND PLURALS

---

Do you have to stop sometimes and wonder whether to use *is* or *are, has* or *have, was* or *were?* Let's discover how easy it is to decide once you're sure of the rules.

---

### *ALL ABOUT SINGULARS AND PLURALS*

*Problem 7.* Neither of his parents *is*—or *are*—alive?
*Solution.* Ask yourself, what word is understood between *neither* and *of* in this problem sentence? Obviously, the word *one.* And do we say, neither one *is,* or neither one *are?* Equally obviously, *is;* hence, neither of his parents *is* alive.

And here we have the important key we need to choose the verb that follows *neither of, either of, each of,* and *one of.*

### Can You Figure Out These Problems?

1. Neither (*one*) of his parents (*has, have?*) arrived.
2. Either (*one*) of the girls (*is, are?*) capable of running the switchboard.
3. Each (*one*) of these reports (*was, were?*) checked.

4. *One* of my best friends (*works, work?*) in your department.

If you noted that we were talking about *one* in these problems, you selected the *first* verb in each case—one *has*, one *is*, etc.

*Problem 8. Has*—or *have*—the manager or his assistant come in yet? *Has*—or *have*—your mother and father arrived?
*Solution.* In the first problem sentence, the correct verb is *has;* but in the second sentence, the correct verb is *have.* Why the difference? Note the rule that applies.

## Rule 6.

When two *singular* subjects are connected by *or* or *nor*, use a *singular* verb; when they are connected by *and*, use a *plural* verb.

## Puzzle Out These Problems:

1. (Has, Have) either your son *or* daughter ever worked here?
2. (Is, Are) there a pen *or* pencil in the drawer?
3. Neither the mechanic *nor* his helper (has, have) come in yet.
4. (Is, Are) your son *and* daughter home today?
5. (Was, Were) the pen *and* pencil in the drawer?

Sentences 1 through 3 have *singular* subjects connected by *or* or *nor*, so the correct verbs are *singular: has, is, has.* In sentences 4 and 5, the connective is *and*, the verb is *plural: are, were.*

*Problem 9. Is*—or *are*—the cost of these items dropping?
*Solution.* What is dropping, the *cost* or the *items*? It's the *cost* (singular), not the *items* (plural); hence, a *singular* verb is required. Correct answer: *is.*

## Rule 7.

When a *singular* subject is followed by *of* and a plural noun, ignore the word after *of*, and make your verb agree with the *singular* subject.

### Puzzle Out These Problems:

1. A *vase* of flowers (is, are) standing on her desk.
2. The first *batch* of items (was, were) defective.
3. Another *collection* of orders (has, have) just come in.
4. The *aim* of all our employees (is, are) to turn out more work.

In each instance, the subject (the word before *of*) is singular—*vase, batch, collection, aim*. Therefore, the correct verb is also singular—*is, was, has, is*.


### *TROUBLESOME PLURALS*

The following words do not end in S; nevertheless they are plurals and should be treated as such.

1. *criteria* (singular, *criterion*)
2. *memoranda* (singular, *memorandum*)
3. *phenomena* (singular, *phenomenon*)

Hence we correctly say, *these* criteria, *those* phenomena, etc.

In the following words (double or hyphenated), we add the *S* to the main elements in order to pluralize them.

| SINGULAR | PLURAL |
| --- | --- |
| mother-in-law | mothers-in-law |
| passer-by | passers-by |
| looker-on | lookers-on |
| attorney general | attorneys general |

But the plurals of solid words such as *spoonful, cupful, handful*, etc., are *spoonfuls, cupfuls, handfuls*, etc.

Are you ready, now, for a complete test of your understanding of singulars and plurals?

**Check Your Learning**

1. Neither of these reports (a–are, b–is) satisfactory.

2. If every one of the employees (a–puts, b–put) in some overtime, we can get the job done in a week.

3. Each of his children (a–have, b–has) managed to go to college.

4. Either the president or the vice-president (a–has, b–have) attended every meeting.

5. The greater size of these machines (a–accounts, b–account) for their staggering cost.

6. He and his sister (a–is, b–are) waiting to see you.

7. (a–Mother-in-laws, b–Mothers-in-law) are rarely as bad as they are painted.

8. (a–That, b–Those) criteria (a–is, b–are) no longer valid.

KEY:   1–b, 2–a, 3–b, 4–a, 5–a, 6–b, 7–b, 8–b, b.


*OTHER WORDS OFTEN CONFUSED*

1. let—leave. *Let* means to *permit*—*let* me go, *let's* not talk about it. *Leave* means to *go away*—*leave* the room, *leave* me alone.

2. hanged-hung. A person is *hanged* when he is put to death by hanging—a picture or other object (or, occasionally, a person) is *hung* when held suspended. The horse thief was *hanged;* they *hanged* the murderer at dawn; we *hung* the picture on the wall.

3. alumnus—alumna. A male graduate of a school is an *alumnus*, a female an *alumna*. The plural of *alumnus* is *alumni* (a-LUM′-nye); the plural of *alumna* is *alumnae* (a-LUM′-nee).

4. incredible—incredulous. A story, thing, or person that *cannot be believed*, i.e., that is *unbelievable*, is *incredible*— an *incredible* account of the night's adventures, an *incredible* witness, etc. A person (and *only* a person) who is *skeptical, unwilling to believe*, is *incredulous*—he looked utterly *incredulous* when he heard the story.

5. beside—besides. *Beside* means *next to*—*beside* the chair. *Besides* means *also, in addition, moreover*, etc. She's not very pretty; *besides*, she has no money.

6. fiancé—fiancée. A man who is engaged to be married is someone's *fiancé* (one E); if it's a woman, she's a *fiancée* (two E's). But both words are pronounced identically—fee-ahn-SAY'.

7. effect—affect. An *effect* is an *idea* or *thing*—a scenic *effect;* what a stunning *effect* she produces; this will have a bad *effect* on production. *Affect*, on the other hand, is a verb meaning to *change, influence, move*, or *pretend*— this will *affect* production; she *affects* everyone strangely; his tears do not *affect* me; he *affected* a southern accent after he returned from Georgia. However, and be careful of this, if your verb has the *special* meaning of *bring about*, spell it *effect*—we shall try to *effect* (bring about) an improvement in production.

## Check Your Learning

1. (a—Let, b—Leave) us go.
2. The thief was (a—hung, b—hanged).
3. These girls are all (a—alumnae, b—alumni) of the same college.
4. He was at first (a—incredible, b—incredulous) when he heard the news.
5. It's too expensive; (a—besides, b—beside), you don't really need it.
6. Her (a—fiancée, b—fiancé) is not very handsome, but he is rich.
7. How does this (a—affect, b—effect) you?

8. That is a strange and unpleasant (a–affect, b–effect).

KEY:    1–a, 2–b, 3–a, 4–b, 5–a, 6–b, 7–a, 8–b.


## *SEE HOW MUCH YOU'VE IMPROVED*

If you have worked conscientiously on Part V, you should be capable now of making a correct and confident choice in most or all of the sentences that follow. You can gauge your progress by the difference in your scores on the two major tests; but bear in mind that any error you make is a signal for careful review.

1. Between you and (a–I, b–me), I think he's completely dishonest.

2. Would you like to come with (a–he and I, b–him and me)?

3. I guess no one can handle this job except (a–her, b–she).

4. Was it (a–she, b–her) who called you?

5. We're not as well paid as (a–them, b–they).

6. You have accomplished more than (a–me, b–I) today.

7. Why don't you invite (a–we, b–us) and the Smiths?

8. (a–Who, b–Whom) do you wish to speak to?

9. (a–Whom, b–Who) did you say won first prize in the Science Fair?

10. Have they (a–hung, be–hanged) the murderer yet?

11. Your attitude (a–effected, b–affected) him strangely.

12. Do you think doctors will ever (a–effect, b–affect) a cure for cancer?

13. Aspirin has an almost immediate (a–affect, b–effect) on him.

14. That story is (a–incredulous, b–incredible).

15. I'd like to (a–lay, b–lie) down for a few minutes.

16. (a–Lay, b–Lie) your coat on the chair.

17. The wounded man (a–laid, b–lied, c–lay) on the street for over an hour before the ambulance arrived.

18. The papers have (a–lain, b–laid) on his desk all day.

19. When either of these calls (a–comes, b–come) in, let me know.

20. Neither of his parents (a–is, b–are) alive.

21. One of his first statements (a–were, b–was) completely wrong.

22. Congress or the President (a–has, b–have) to tackle this job.

23. The price of these books (a–is, b–are) considerably higher than last year.

24. (a–Is, b–Are) your sister and brother home from school yet?

25. (a–Those, b–That) memoranda (a–are, b–is) not what we want.

KEY:   1–b, 2–b, 3–a, 4–a, 5–b, 6–b, 7–b, 8–b, 9–b, 10–b, 11–b, 12–a, 13–b, 14–b, 15–b, 16–a, 17–c, 18–a, 19–a, 20–a, 21–b, 22–a, 23–a, 24–b, 25–a, a.

# Twenty-fifth Day

## JUST FOR FUN (V)

### I. THOSE PESKY PRONOUNS!

Pronouns are the most troublesome words in the English language. Actual tests have shown that these one-syllable tricksters pop up incorrectly in everyday speech more often than four- and five-syllable tongue twisters. *I* or *me*? *He* or *him*? *We* or *us*? *She* or *her*? *They* or *them*? *Who* or *whom*? Even experts stumble over these. Where do you stand? Try the following. Eleven or more correct make your pronouns pets instead of pests.

1. Where can you find a better teacher than (*he, him*)?
2. No one except (*she, her*) can help you.
3. Let's keep this strictly between you and (*I, me*).
4. The baby looks more like (*I, me*) every day.
5. Everyone agreed to the change but (*we, us*).
6. Was it (*they, them*) the letter referred to?
7. Under these circumstances, how would you like to be (*we, us*)?
8. He wants you and (*I, me*) to come to the party.
9. How would you like to have dinner with my parents and (*I, me*)?
10. We are as good as (*they, them*) any day.
11. What would the girls do without (*we, us*) boys?
12. (*Who, whom*) would you like to be if you were not yourself?

13. He is the only judge (*who, whom*) we think is capable of conducting the trial.

14. We will work with (*whoever, whomever*) has been assigned to teach the class.

KEY: 1—he, 2—her, 3—me, 4—me, 5—us, 6—they, 7—we, 8—me, 9—me, 10—they, 11—us, 12—who, 13—who, 14—whoever.

## II. PROUD OF YOUR PAST?

Can you write the correct past and perfect tenses of the following verbs?

| | *Example:* | *Past* | *Perfect* |
|---|---|---|---|
| | write | wrote | has written |
| 1. | flee | _____ | _____ |
| 2. | fly | _____ | _____ |
| 3. | drink | _____ | _____ |
| 4. | swim | _____ | _____ |
| 5. | hang (a criminal) | _____ | _____ |
| 6. | lay | _____ | _____ |
| 7. | lie | _____ | _____ |
| 8. | lead | _____ | _____ |
| 9. | strive | _____ | _____ |

KEY: 1—fled, fled; 2—flew, flown; 3—drank, drunk; 4—swam (or swum), swum; 5—hanged, hanged; 6—laid, laid; 7—lay, lain; 8—led, led; 9—strove, striven.

## III. WHAT DO YOU KNOW ABOUT SEX?

Can you write the correct feminine form of each of the following words?

| | | | |
|---|---|---|---|
| 1. bachelor | _____ | 7. horse | _____ |
| 2. baron | _____ | 8. maharajah | _____ |
| 3. beau | _____ | 9. marquis | _____ |
| 4. buck | _____ | 10. wizard | _____ |
| 5. drake | _____ | 11. sire | _____ |
| 6. earl | _____ | 12. sultan | _____ |

KEY: 1—spinster, 2—baroness, 3—belle, 4—doe, 5—duck, 6—countess, 7—mare, 8—maharani, 9—marchioness, 10—witch, 11—dam, 12—sultana.

## IV. WHAT DO YOU KNOW ABOUT BABIES?

A baby dog is a *puppy;* a baby cat is a *kitten.* Do you know what each of the following is called when it's a baby?

| | |
|---|---|
| 1. bear | _____ |
| 2. cod | _____ |
| 3. deer | _____ |
| 4. duck | _____ |
| 5. elephant | _____ |
| 6. goose | _____ |
| 7. hen | _____ |
| 8. sheep | _____ |
| 9. mare | _____ |
| 10. horse | _____ |

KEY: 1—cub, 2—codling, 3—fawn, 4—duckling, 5—calf, 6—gosling, 7—chick or pullet, 8—lamb, 9—filly, 10—colt or foal.

## V. WHAT DO YOU KNOW ABOUT PLURALS?

Almost all English words are pluralized by the simple process of adding -S or -ES. But not the following ten—so can you put on your thinking cap and give the correct plural for each word?

1. insigne          _____
2. libretto         _____
3. madame           _____
4. locus            _____
5. larva            _____
6. datum            _____
7. analysis         _____
8. alumnus          _____
9. alumna           _____
10. criterion       _____

KEY:   1—insignia,  2—libretti,  3—mesdames,  4—loci,  5—larvae,  6—data,  7—analyses,  8—alumni,  9—alumnae, 10—criteria.

## VI. WHAT DO YOU KNOW ABOUT GROUPS?

Animals, things, people are often found in distinctive groups—and each group has a special name, depending on its composition. Can you write the word which properly describes a group of each of the following?

1. puppies         _____
2. ants            _____
3. actors          _____
4. wolves          _____
5. goats           _____
6. fish            _____
7. bees            _____
8. chicks          _____
9. worshipers      _____
10. stars          _____

KEY: 1–litter, 2–colony, 3–troupe or company, 4–pack, 5–flock, 6–school or shoal, 7–colony, hive, or swarm, 8–brood, 9–congregation, 10–constellation.

# PART VI

# *The Modern View of Correctness in English*

"Correctness" is determined by present-day educated usage. But how is such usage determined? Part VI first explains how surveys are conducted among professional users of the language, then goes on to cover a number of random problems in grammar that possibly you've often wondered about.

# Twenty-sixth Day

## HOW CORRECT MUST CORRECT ENGLISH BE?

---

An informal investigation for *Harper's Magazine* that turned up some surprising results.

---

"Even if you do learn to speak correct English," the late Clarence Darrow once remarked, "who are you going to speak it to?" According to an informal sampling which I made recently for *Harper's Magazine*, you would do best speaking it to the editors of women's magazines. On the other hand, your *least* receptive audience, if you restricted your speech to rigidly formal grammatical patterns, would be college professors of English.

With the co-operation of the editors of *Harper's*, I sent to nine different groups of people a questionnaire consisting of nineteen sentences. In each sentence a controversial grammatical expression was underlined, with space provided for indicating approval or disapproval of the usage. Instructions for answering the questionnaire were as follows:

"Here are nineteen expressions about which there is today a good deal of controversy, and we'd like your opinion, as an educated adult, of their acceptability in everyday speech.

"Do not be influenced by whether these usages do or do not violate formal grammatical rules. Rather, indicate, by an affirmative vote, that you would be willing to use the expression listed or that you believe such an expression has become sufficiently current in educated American speech to be labeled acceptable usage; by a negative vote, that the expression, as used, is unacceptable in educated circles."

## THE 19 SENTENCES

1. His attitude makes me *mad*. (*Mad* as a synonym for *angry*).
2. I *will* pay your bill if you accept my check.
3. The reason I'm worried is *because* I think she's ill.
4. His work is different *than* mine.
5. We had a *nice* time at the party.
6. *Can* I have another helping of dessert, please?
7. I encountered *less* difficulties than I had expected.
8. Everyone put on *their coats* and went home.
9. How much money have you *got*?
10. *Due* to the storm, all trains are late.
11. She has an *awful* headache.
12. We *only* have five left.
13. Let's not walk any *further* right now.
14. We must remember *to accurately check* each answer.
15. He's one person I simply won't do business *with*.
16. Go *slow*.
17. It is *me*.
18. She acts as if she *was* my wife.
19. *Who* did you meet?

Above you will find the sentences as they were presented on the questionnaire. You may wish to cast a vote for or against each one, so that you will be able later to compare your own conservatism or liberalism, grammatically speaking, with the reactions of the nine groups of educated adults who were polled.

Four hundred sixty-eight people, out of 750 to whom I wrote, answered the questionnaire. Ballots were received from high school and college teachers of English, authors, editors, journalists, radio commentators, lexicographers, and a random sampling of subscribers to *Harper's Magazine*.

Each respondent cast 19 votes, apportioning them as he saw fit between acceptance or rejection of the usages questioned. I have subsequently worked out what might be called the "acceptance ratio" for each group of people—the percentage of affirmative votes to total votes cast by members of that group. I realize that the number of people in some of these groups was small and that therefore no vast significance should be attached to their "acceptance ratios" (which I shall shorten to A.R.'s); but you may be interested to know how the various groups ranked in the liberalism-conservatism scale.

The most liberal group—the one most inclined to accept these usages—was composed of 155 college teachers of English, who piled up an aggregate A.R. of 70. (This result certainly disproves the recurrent rumors that professors are stuffy, musty, pedantic, and unrealistic.) Out of a total of 2945 votes cast, 19 to each professor, only 891 were negative. A majority of the professors accepted 17 of the 19 sentences, rejecting only "His work is different *than* mine" (No. 4) and "I encountered *less* difficulties than I had expected" (No. 7); and a sizable number of professors voted a straight affirmative ticket. The following professorial comments are typical of many:

"By direct observation, I have noticed that all of these usages are actually used by speakers who are socially and intellectually acceptable." (A Cornell University professor).

"If the criterion for 'good English' is usage—and certainly no other criterion makes any sense—then all of these expression are either acceptable now or will be within the next few decades." (Professor at State University of Iowa.)

The next most liberal group was composed of the lexicographers, 12 in number, with an A.R. of 65. They included members of the editorial staffs of all standard American dictionaries.

The 33 authors and the 80 editors (these represented the staffs of book publishing houses as well as of general magazines) ran so close for third position that their differences had to be calculated to two decimal places— 56.14 for the authors, 56.11 for the editors. Next in order came the radio columnists, 22 in number with an A.R. of 51.7, then the 32 high school teachers of English, with an A.R. of 51.4. (Half or more of the latter voted affirmatively for only 9 of the usages. It was noteworthy that those from small towns were significantly more conservative than those from large cities; and many were vociferous in their remarks about the need for preserving strict grammatical standards.)

A sampling of *Harper's* subscribers throughout the nation brought 60 responses from readers of varied occupations and professions; they turned in an A.R. of precisely 50. Forty-eight feature writers and columnists on several New York newspapers and one Chicago daily made a still stricter showing, with an A.R. of only 47. And the most conservative of all the groups was a collection of 26 editors of women's magazines, with 45. Originally I had planned to group all the editors in one category, but as the early returns began to come in it was evident that the editors of women's magazines were much stricter in their attitudes toward everyday speech than were their opposite numbers on the general magazines. I leave it to the sociologists to account for the discrepancy.

\* \* \*

Now let us see how the votes ran on the 19 individual expressions in the questionnaire. In each case I have determined the percentage of acceptance among the respondents *as a whole*, somewhat arbitrarily labeling any expression that received an affirmative vote of 75 percent or more as ESTABLISHED ENGLISH; any expression that received between 50 and 75 percent acceptance as ACCEPTABLE ENGLISH; any expression that received less than 50 percent acceptance but more than 35 percent as CONTROVERSIAL; and any that failed to receive as much as 35 percent acceptance as REJECTED. There is some temptation, of course, to give extra weight to the opinions of the professors and lexicographers, as these gentlemen maintain a closer touch with historical trends in grammar than do the members of the other groups. But it must be borne in mind that the grammatical attitudes of the general educated populace depend not alone upon the findings of experts but also upon the influence of those groups whose language patterns are constantly in the public eye and ear, such as authors, editors, and radio and television speakers. (Proof of this fact lies in the middle-of-the-road voting of the 60 subscribers to *Harper's*.) And one must also remember that high school teachers do more to condition the attitudes of the general public than do professors of English, because there are so many more of them. So I am not inclined to load the scales in favor of the experts, and will therefore count any vote as equal to any other, regardless of its source.

Here, then, is the way the score runs, expression by expression:

*No. 1*. His attitude makes me *mad*. ACCEPTABLE ENGLISH. Acceptance, 68 percent.

Recent editions of dictionaries concede that *mad* is

acceptable colloquially as a synonym for *angry* and over two thirds of the respondents agreed. One hundred seventeen of the 155 professors and 9 of the 12 lexicographers voted affirmatively on the sentence. The high school teachers, however, rejected the usage by a vote of 18 to 14—the only group in which a majority turned in a negative response.

*Random Comment:*

"Only the purists shun *mad* in familiar speech." (General magazine editor.)

"I would use *mad* for *angry* except in the most pedantic of situations and in instances where the meaning of *mad* might be ambiguous." (Professor at Northwestern University.)

*No. 2.* I *will* pay your bill if you accept my check. ESTABLISHED ENGLISH. Acceptance, 90 percent.

The ancient and outmoded distinction between *shall* and *will* found favor only among 46 of the 468 respondents; 149 out of 155 professors and every one of the 12 lexicographers accepted the use of *will* with *I*, even though no "determination" is expressed by the sentence. (The highest numerical *negative* vote came from the *Harper's* subscribers, 11 out of 60, the next highest from the newspaper writers, 10 out of 48.)

*Random Comment:*

"The fact is that *shall* is simply going out of business." (Well-known novelist.)

"The insistence on *shall* with the first person is an invention of the schoolmarms; it has never been an essential of good English." (Professor at Cornell University.)

"The distinction between *shall* and *will* is rapidly becoming obsolete." (Lexicographer.)

No. 3. The reason I'm worried is *because* I think she's ill. CONTROVERSIAL. Acceptance, 48 percent.

The respondents as a whole rejected this usage in a close vote: 245 to 223. It is significant, however, that a comfortable majority of the professors (89 to 66) accepted this common substitution of *because* where strict grammar requires *that*. The question split the lexicographers evenly (6 to 6) and had the same effect on the *Harper's* subscribers (30 to 30). In all other groups the usage lost out, though generally by a narrow margin, except for the women's magazine editors and newspaper writers, in which groups the vote went against it in a ratio of approximately 2 to 1.

*Random Comment:*

"On the whole, the writer should judge by the sound of a sentence. Incorrect grammar leads to awkward-sounding sentences. 'Is because' is an example of this." (Associate editor of a general magazine.)
"*Because* meets with a good bit of resistance in my circles, but it is certainly growing in favor in the spoken language." (Professor at Atlanta University.)

No. 4. His work is different *than* mine. REJECTED. Acceptance, 31 percent.

This usage failed to get majority approval from a single group, though paradoxically enough the radio people, generally far down in the liberalism-conservatism scale, split their vote exactly evenly, 11 to 11. This was one of the only two sentences rejected by the professors, who voted against *different than* by 93 to 62.

\* \* \*

*No. 5.* We had a *nice* time at the party, ESTABLISHED ENGLISH. Acceptance, 88 percent.

The professors accepted this usage by a vote of 144 to 11, the lexicographers by a vote of 10 to 2, and the radio people, again paradoxically, backed it unanimously. Greatest conservatism on this point was indicated by the high school teachers; over 28 percent of them rejected the use of *nice* to mean *agreeable* or *pleasant.*

*Random Comment:*

"*Nice time* is a good American colloquialism." (A novelist.)

*No. 6. Can* I have another helping of dessert, please? CONTROVERSIAL. Acceptance, 40 percent.

The use of *can* to ask permission found favor in the eyes of 185 of the 468 respondents. Only the professors gave it a majority vote (87 to 68), but there was a fair proportion of support in the other groups. The greatest conservatism on this point was shown by the newspaper writers, who voted against it in a ratio of better than 3 to 1.

*No. 7.* I encountered *less* difficulties than I had expected. REJECTED. Acceptance, 23 percent.

Though *less* frequently accompanies a plural noun on educated levels of speech and in the writing of educated authors, the voting went against the usage in all groups, including the professors, only 49 of the 155 accepting it. Among the other respondents, the ratio of rejection went as high in many groups as 7 to 1.

*No. 8.* Everyone put on *their coats* and went home. CONTROVERSIAL. Acceptance, 45 percent.

It is especially indicative of the generally liberal tendencies of educated people that this clear-cut violation of grammatical agreement should have fared as well as it did. In logic, *everyone*, *everybody*, and similar "singular" pronouns have a strong plural meaning, and it takes a good deal of linguistic sophistication to keep agreement uniform without sounding like a product of a night school class in diction. Carried to its illogical extreme, formal grammar requires that *everyone* be followed by *him* or *his* even in curious sentences like the following:

"Since *everyone* in the room spoke Spanish, I addressed *him* in that language."

"As soon as *everyone* was finished, we started collecting *his* paper."

These sentences as they stand are grammatically "pure"—they are also logically insane, and I submit that only a die-hard purist would avoid *them* or *their* in such constructions.

The vote of the 468 respondents went against the usage in question by 259 to 209. Only the professors gave it a majority vote, 93 to 62. All other groups rejected it, the lexicographers by a close vote of 7 to 5, the women's magazine editors by a ratio of almost 2½ to 1.

*No. 9.* How much money have you *got*? ACCEPTABLE ENGLISH. Acceptance, 65 percent.

One hundred thirty-one of the 155 professors accepted his popular usage, but the other groups were less liberally inclined. Fifty-five percent of *Harper's* subscribers and 57 percent of the women's magazine editors voted against it.

*Random Comment:*

"Historically this is good usage." (Professor at Colorado A. and M. College.)

"A trifle barbarous, perhaps, but so universally used as to be forgivable." (Well-known author.)

"Fully established; more emphatic than 'How much money have you?'." (A professor of English.)

No. 10. *Due* to the storm all trains are late. ACCEPTABLE ENGLISH. Acceptance, 65 percent.

*Due to*, as a preposition, received a majority affirmative vote from all groups, including the women's magazine editors.

*Random Comments:*

"Useless to fight; it is established." (A lexicographer.)
" 'Due to' in the sense of 'owing to' has been in good usage for two hundred years or longer." (Another lexicographer.)

No. 11. She has an *awful* headache. ESTABLISHED ENGLISH. Acceptance, 77 percent.

The 12 lexicographers voted unanimously for this usage, and over 83 percent of the professors. Thirty-three percent of the high school teachers rejected it and about 30 percent of *Harper's* subscribers.

No. 12. We *only* have five left. CONTROVERSIAL. Acceptance, 44 percent.

It is a little surprising, I think, that this usage fared as poorly as it did. I have rarely heard even the most erudite of people, unless they were speaking with studied formality, place *only* in its grammatical position (before the word it actually limits) rather than in its natural and popular position (before the verb). It is true, of course, that written and edited English shifts *only* to the position which the stricter grammarians insist upon, and in manuscripts prepared for the printer I am sure that this innocent adverb is circled and arrowed more than any other word in the English language.

Nevertheless, despite the emphasis in the introduction to the ballot that this was a poll on *speech*, the vote went against the usage of 265 to 203. The professors, of course, accepted the sentence, by a vote of 97 to 58; the lexicographers were split evenly, 6 to 6. Other groups, however, turned it down in varying ratios: editors by 5 to 3, radio people by 3 to 1, women's magazine editors by 3 to 1, and newspaper writers by almost 4 to 1.

*No. 13.* Let's not walk any *further* right now. ACCEPTABLE ENGLISH. Acceptance, 56 percent.

Strict rule requires *farther* in reference to spatial distance, although the dictionaries now record that *further* is used in reference either to degree or to distance. Eleven lexicographers and 104 professors accepted the sentence; the authors favored the usage with a bare majority of 1. More than half the radio people, newspaper writers, and women's magazine editors voted against it.

*Random Comment:*

"This distinction has broken down completely." (Professor at Pomona College.)
"As applied to spatial distance, *further* and *farther* have long been interchangeable." (A lexicographer.)
"*Further* and *farther* are hardly distinguishable in ordinary fluid talk." (Professor at Pratt Institute.)

*No. 14.* We must remember *to accurately check* each answer. ACCEPTABLE ENGLISH. Acceptance, 53 percent.

A number of respondents noted that they accepted the split infinitive in principle but preferred to vote against this one as awkward and unnecessary, since *accurately*, in their opinion, could come just as satisfactorily at the end of the sentence. Whether voting on principle or in regard to the specific sentence, only the professors, general editors, and lexicographers rolled up a group-majority vote in favor. The women's magazine editors rejected the sentence by a vote of over 2½ to 1.

*Random Comment:*

"I would like to defend the split infinitive. The structure adds strength to the sentence—it is compact and clear. The adverb, sewn and riveted to the verb that way, cannot possibly modify anything but its own verb. This is to loudly say that I split an infinitive whenever I can catch one." (General magazine editor.)

"The restriction against the split infinitive is, to my mind, the most artificial of all grammatical rules. I find that most educated people today split infinitives regularly in their speech and only eliminate them from their writing when they rewrite and polish their material. The only reason they do so is because they were so taught in elementary school." (Editor of one of the largest publishing houses.)

*No. 15.* He's one person I simply won't do business *with*. ESTABLISHED ENGLISH. Acceptance, 86 percent.

That few sane people trouble themselves very much about the heinousness of ending a sentence with a preposition is indicated by the overwhelming majority of acceptance for sentence 15. The radio people, however, voted almost 41 percent against it.

*Random Comment:*

"This has been a dead issue for so many years that I am amazed to see it still classed as controversial." (A lexicographer.)

*No. 16.* Go *slow*. ESTABLISHED ENGLISH. Acceptance, 84 percent.

*Slow* is both an adverb and an adjective, as any dictionary will attest, and only a purist finds any fault with this popular usage. A mere 75 of the 468 respondents rejected the expression, among whom are counted almost 36 percent of the radio people, 28 percent of *Harper's* subscribers, and 33 percent of the newspaper writers.

*No. 17.* It is *me.* ACEPTABLE ENGLISH. Acceptance, 62 percent.

Seventy-seven percent of the professors, 75 percent of the lexicographers, and almost 82 percent of the authors accepted this popular "violation" of strict grammatical rule. The majority of *Harper's* subscribers, newspaper writers, and women's magazine editors, however, rejected it. Among the high school teachers the vote was close: 17 for 15, against.

*No. 18.* She acts as if she *was* my wife. REJECTED. Acceptance, 34 percent.

That the obsolescent subjunctive mood is holding on tenaciously, at least in contrary-to-fact conditions such as this one, is evident from the balloting. Though the mood itself is fast falling into disuse in modern English, its popularity after the conjunction *if* seems to be gaining—and you will often hear it used even where the "rules" do not require it. Especially in the phrase "If I *were* you" it occurs almost universally in educated speech.

There was an interesting contrast in the way the groups voted on this sentence. Three groups—the professors, the lexicographers, and the authors—accepted the sentence by clear-cut majorities, the authors by the ratio of over 5 to 1. The other groups, on the contrary, voted against it overwhelmingly, the general editors and high school teachers in the ratio of better than 2 to 1, the radio people 10 to 1, and the editors of women's magazines, by a vociferous 12 to 1.

*No. 19. Who* did you meet? CONTROVERSIAL. Acceptance, 43 percent.

The growing tendency by all classes of educated speakers to use the nominative *who* as the first word in a sentence, even though grammatically it functions as an object, is attested by the large vote recorded in its favor on the ballots, 200 out of 468. (The scholarly Oxford Dictionary, by the way, defines *whom* as the objective case of *who,* "no longer current in natural colloquial speech.") The professors, lexicographers, and authors gave it a majority vote of acceptance, but in the more conservative groups it was voted down: 24 to 8 among the high school teachers, 33 to 15 among newspaper writers, and 19 to 7 among women's magazine editors.

*Random Comments:*

"Center your attention exclusively on No. 19. The most loathsome word (to me at least) in the English language is 'whom.' You can always tell a half-educated buffoon by the care he takes in working the word in. When he starts it I know I am faced with a pompous illiterate who is not going to have me long as company." (General magazine editor.)

Although this sampling of educated opinion on matters of usage is, to my knowledge, the largest ever taken, I do not pretend that it is definitive or that it settles any questions beyond possible cavil. I think the results indicate with a fair degree of accuracy the comparative linguistic liberalism of those groups of citizens who use the English language as a direct means of earning a livelihood. I think also that we are justified in accepting the final tabulations as incontrovertible proof that English grammar is far more fluid and less restrictive than some "speech manuals" and textbooks admit or than many nonprofessional people realize. It is certainly obvious that "correct" and "incorrect" are subtle, intangible, and relative terms when applied to informal educated speech, and that reverential adherence to hidebound grammatical "rules" is not a characteristic of the educated speaker in America.

# *Twenty-seventh Day*

## HOW WOULD YOU SOLVE THESE FIVE GRAMMAR PROBLEMS?

*Like* or *as? Me* or *I?* None *are* or none *is? Between* or *among* three dresses? How do *you* usually say it, and are you right or wrong?

Come right down to it, there's nothing we notice so quickly (nor, sometimes, with such ill-concealed delight) as the other fellow's mistakes. And, of course, there's nothing we're usually so blind to as our own errors.

This all-too-human reaction occurs just as regularly in respect to the use of words as it does in regard to dress, table manners, or morals.

But when it comes to English, we must bear in mind that any living language is a tricky business. Knowing formal principles is often only the first step; for while grammatical rules are stable enough, actual observance of them varies from time to time and from place to place. So there is a second step to take—namely, realizing that "correctness" is a highly relative and changeable term, that yesterday's error has a very good chance of being today's acceptable usage.

Here are some notes on modern trends in grammar that will keep you right up to the minute. They have been prepared by polling four selected groups of people who use the English language professionally—33 editors, 7 book reviewers, 31 well-known authors, and 11 professors of English in leading American universities.

Check up on your own speech by deciding whether the italicized words in the test sentences are perfectly correct for everyday usage or whether they are far enough removed from good English to be marked "doubtful." Then compare your views with the opinions offered in the explanatory paragraphs that follow the test.

### TEST YOURSELF

*Correct  Doubtful*

1. He's not doing his work *like* I told him to.    _____  _____

2. He acts more like you and *I* every day.    _____  _____

3. None of the houses *are* cheap enough.    _____  _____

4. She is having difficulty choosing *between* the three dresses.    _____  _____

5. "Are you going to invite Bob and Dorothy?" *"Sure!"*    _____  _____

1. He's not doing his work *like* I told him to. *DOUBTFUL.*

What possible objection can there be to the word *like* as it appears in our test sentence? Notice the verb *told*—formal grammar claims that *like* is a preposition, and therefore may not be followed by a verb. In a construction like this one, says the rule, *as* or *as if* should be substituted, depending on which conjunction fits.

Many educated speakers have a deep-seated aversion to *like* before a verb, and in the poll the vote was 62 against the test sentence, only 20 for. Ilka Chase, noted author and actress, made this typical comment on her questionnaire: "I realize that this use of the word *like* is commonplace, but to my way of thinking it is inexcusable, marking the speaker as grossly uneducated."

One must admit, nevertheless, that *like* with a verb is fairly prevalent, particularly in the southern and western states of the nation. Harry S Truman, a true Missourian in his speech patterns, described his reaction to the news of Franklin Roosevelt's sudden death in the following terms: "I felt *like* the moon, the stars, and all the planets had fallen on me."

And perhaps you have heard of the song that Eddie Cantor made so popular: "If you knew Suzie *like* I know Suzie," not to mention the commercial, "Winstons taste good *like* a cigarette should."

Everything considered, and weighing all the pros and cons, I think we must conclude that *like* before a verb is still a controversial, though not necessarily uneducated, usage. To be 100 percent safe, and to avoid any possibility of criticism, it is probably wise to stick to *as* or *as if* in formal speech and writing.

2.  He acts more like you and *I* every day. *DOUBTFUL*.

Here we are dealing with a usage which isn't a bit controversial. Since *like* is not followed by a verb, it is functioning in this sentence as a standard, honest-to-goodness preposition—as such, it is perferably used with *me*, an objective pronoun, rather than *I*, a nominative pronoun. Phrases like "between you and *I*," "like you and *I*," "except you and *I*," etc. (*between, like, except* are prepositions), are rarely, if ever, heard in educated speech. Correct form: He acts more like you and *me* every day.

3.  None of the houses *are* cheap enough. *CORRECT*.

In many newspapers and in a good deal of formal

writing, you will find *none* used with a *singular* verb. If you have noticed this phenomenon and been puzzled by it, you will be relieved to learn that the usage is based on an antiquated principle of English grammar. This outmoded rule holds that since *none* originally meant *not one* it must always be considered singular in form. Maybe it is singular in *form*, but it is sometimes so obviously plural in *meaning* that in all good sense we cannot, I submit, insist on using it only with a singular verb. This opinion is corroborated by the respondents to the poll, who accepted the test sentence by a vote of 73 to 9. When Sterling Andrus Leonard, until his recent death Professor of English at Wisconsin University, made a survey of current English usage for the National Council of Teachers of English, he concluded that "none . . . are" is established English. Professor Leonard quoted one authority as saying, "It is pure priggishness to pretend that *none* is always singular."

It all boils down to this: In expressions like "none of the houses," "None of the girls," etc., the implication is strongly plural. Feel perfectly free, therefore, to use a plural verb.

4. She's having difficulty choosing *between* the three dresses. *CORRECT*.

"*Between* for two things, *among* for three or more" is a rule honored by tradition but, more often than not, ignored in actual usage. The American College Dictionary says that in instances "in which each object is individually related to the rest, *between* is used of more than two," and the Merriam-Webster Collegiate Dictionary, making the same point, offers as an example: "The three survivors had but one pair of shoes *between* them."

Weighing the merits of each dress against each of the others, the young lady is making a choice *between* the three dresses; to use *among* in this sentence would, I think, sound awkward and ridiculously stilted. In any similar situation, *between* is absolutely correct, even if more than two things are involved.

This sentence was accepted by the overwhelming ratio of 71 to 11.

5. "Are you going to invite Bob and Dorothy?" *"Sure!"* CORRECT.

There was very little disagreement among the judges on this usage. The college professors and book reviewers accepted it unanimously, and only 6 authors and 3 editors cast negative votes. It is a common American tendency to shorten adverbs—*Go slow*, for example, is more popular than *Go slowly*. And "Sure!" as an enthusiastic answer to a question is at least as acceptable as "Surely!", though "Surely!" may have a politer and somewhat more formal air. I think it is especially inadvisable and certainly unrealistic for parents to correct children who are in the habit of responding "Sure!" to a request. Youngsters are linguistically very imitative and pick up expressions from their social environment; forcing a child to say "Surely!" when he does not normally do so will make his speech conspicuous and perhaps tend to reduce his popularity among his friends. Considering the opinions of the professional people who responded to the poll, "Surely!" vs. "Sure!" is far less important than some parents seem to think.

# Twenty-eighth Day

## SEVEN NEW PROBLEMS TO PIT YOUR WITS AGAINST

---

Is a singular or plural verb used after *who?* What is the difference between *childlike* and *childish?* When do you feel *bad*, when *badly?* Which is correct, *we* boys or *us* boys? More excursions into the kind of pesky little problems that make English so difficult.

---

If you have an idea that English is a difficult, subtle, and complicated language, full of pitfalls and booby traps for the unwary, let me assure you that you are 100 percent right.

Even though grammar is today considerably more liberal than ever before, certain pesky problems continually arise in a active day's conversation. For instance: When do you *feel bad* and when do you *feel badly?* Is innocence *childish* or is it *childlike?* Should you say *we girls* or *us girls?* And so on, almost without end.

Pit your wits against some problems that are likely to confront you in your own everyday speech—see how often you can come to a proper decision without doubt or hesitation.

## TEST YOURSELF

|  | Right | Wrong |
|---|---|---|
| 1. It is I who *is* responsible for his safety. | _____ | _____ |
| 2. She is one of those girls who *flirts* with all the boys in the class. | _____ | _____ |
| 3. Do you like *these* insignia? | _____ | _____ |
| 4. Joan has a *childlike* innocence that is most refreshing. | _____ | _____ |
| 5. I feel *badly* about your illness. | _____ | _____ |
| 6. *Us* boys certainly stole a march on the girls that time! | _____ | _____ |
| 7. You can't talk that way to *we* girls. | _____ | _____ |

1. It is I who *is* responsible for his safety. *WRONG*.

Here we have an extremely bookish, not to say downright erudite, way of expressing oneself. The generality of people would happily settle for "I am the one who is responsible for his safety," and thereby avoid a nasty grammatical pitfall; so if you insist on couching the thought in more scholarly language you had better stick to strict grammar and say "It is I who *am* responsible for his safety." *Who* is a pronoun of changeable nature, taking whatever verb is required by its "antecedent"—that is, the word it refers to—which in this sentence is *I*. Since *I* is naturally followed by *am*, so also is *who* in the usage under discussion. The pattern is *I who am, you who are, he who is, one who is*, and so on right down the line.

2. She is one of those girls who *flirts* with all the boys in the class. *WRONG*.

*Who*, as we decided in Problem 1, takes the verb required by its antecedent, which in this case is *girls*. Girls *flirt*; therefore, "She is one of those *girls* who *flirt* with all the boys in the class." Or you may wish to apply a test of logic. *She is one of those girls.* Which girls? *Those girls who flirt with all the boys in the class.* Grammatically or logically, *flirt* is the proper form.

3. Do you like *these* insignia? *RIGHT*.

*Insignia* is, technically speaking, a plural word, though I doubt that one person out of a hundred knows its singular form, *insigne*, pronounced in-SIG'-nee. (This piece of information will give you a decided advantage over your most intellectual friends.) To be superlatively correct, we should say either "*This insigne is* most impressive" or "*These insignia are* most impressive." But to be realistic, we must recognize that *insignia*, which neither looks nor sounds like a conventional plural noun, is being very widely used as a singular in cultivated speech.

4. Joan has a *childlike* innocence that is most refreshing. *RIGHT*.

The sense of this sentence is complimentary—the speaker is implying, by means of the adjective *refreshing*, that he finds the sophistication of most girls somewhat tiresome and is glad to have found one girl who still possesses the unsullied innocence of childhood. *Childlike* and *childish* are essentially the same in meaning—it is their emotional flavors are different. *Childish* indicates a derogatory attitude; *childish* fear, *childish* stubbornness, *childish* temper, etc. *Childlike*, on the other hand, is used to describe characteristics which are considered admirable: *childlike* innocence, *childlike* charm, *childlike* trust.

5. I feel *badly* about your illness. *RIGHT*.

You may wonder what objection anyone can have to this sentence, but a quick inspection of some of the older grammar manuals will show that this use of *badly* was once darkly frowned upon. Why? Because the verb *feel*, according to strict rule, takes the adjective *bad*, not the adverb *badly*. Comparison is made with "It feels *soft*" (not *softly*) and "I feel *sick*" (not *sickly*).

However, strict rules do not always hold in educated speech—and to indicate mental distress, many cultivated people habitually say "I feel *badly*," perhaps because such phrasing has none of the implication of wickedness or mischievousness that might be understood from "I feel *bad*."

6. *Us* boys certainly stole a march on the girls that time! *WRONG*.

Although no literate person in his right mind ever uses the pronoun *us* as a subject of a verb, *us boys* in the same capacity may not sound too impossible to the unsophisticated ear. Hence the problem.

If you are ever in doubt about whether to say *we* or *us* in a situation like this, think of the sentence without the noun which follows the doubtful pronoun. By this means you will be able to resist any temptation to choose the incorrect form. Proper usage: "*We* certainly stole a march . . ." Therefore, "*We* boys certainly stole a march . . ."

7. You can't talk that way to *we* girls. *WRONG*.

The sentence without the noun *girls* will indicate the proper usage: "You can't talk that way to *us*." Therefore, "You can't talk that way to *us* girls."

# *Twenty-ninth Day*

## NINE FINAL PROBLEMS AND HOW TO TACKLE THEM

---

When are we *disinterested*, when *uninterested*? Is *phenomenon* singular or plural? How about *measles, mathematics*? Is it all right to use *due to* as a conjunction? Is *try and come* good English? Is *older than me* correct English? And is thick hair *luxurious* or *luxuriant*? Some more notes on present-day educated standards in American English.

---

No doubt you have heard about the woman who stopped at the meat counter of a supermarket.

"A pound of kiddlies, please," she said.

The butcher stared at his customer in disbelief. Collecting his wits at last, he inquired hopefully, "Don't you mean *kidneys*, madam?"

The answer was immediate and very much annoyed. "Well, I *said* kiddlies, did'll I?"

The classic story about the New York urchin illustrates the same point.

The boy was sitting in his third-grade classroom one sunny spring day when a sparrow lighted on the window sill.

"Teacher! Teacher!" he screamed in delight. "Look! A boid!"

"No, Johnnie," said the teacher, who for months had been wearily struggling to correct the children's English. "That's not a *boid*—it's a *bird*."

"Oh." The child was crestfallen and more than a little puzzled. "It sure *looks* like a boid."

As you see, you can't always trust your own ears. Expressions which you use habitually may sound perfect to you—but what do your listeners think of them? On the other hand, certain usages that are quite common in educated circles, and therefore 100 percent correct English, may offend you.

Some of the sentences in the following test are good English. Others would rarely, if ever, be heard in cultivated speech. Check up on your own language patterns by marking each italicized expression right or wrong, then compare your reactions to the opinions given in the explanations.

## TEST YOURSELF

|  | Right | Wrong |
|---|---|---|
| 1. I'm sorry, but I'm *disinterested* in your problems. | | |
| 2. The reason she's fat is *because* she eats too much. | | |
| 3. It's *a phenomena*, that's what it is! | | |
| 4. Measles *is* catching. | | |
| 5. Mathematics *are* a fascinating subject. | | |
| 6. *Due* to a bad cold, he stayed home. | | |
| 7. Please *try and* come early. | | |
| 8. She's much older than *me*. | | |
| 9. Don't you envy her *luxurious* black hair? | | |

1. I'm sorry, but I'm *disinterested* in your problems. *WRONG*.

Do you think that disinterested is a more elegant and more erudite way of saying *uninterested*? Then you are laboring under a misconception.

If you're bored by discussions of early Roman civilization, you're *uninterested*. If you're indifferent to the blandishments of the canvasser at your door and would rather get back to your housework than listen to his sales talk, you're still *uninterested*.

Then when are you *disinterested*? Only when you are neutral, unbiased, or not personally involved in an issue. Two people who have a dispute often go to a third, *disinterested*, party for an objective and impartial opinion. Judges are required by law to be *disinterested* in the cases tried before them—it would be most unfortunate for all concerned, however, if they were also *uninterested*.

In short, the two words have different meanings. Don't use one when you mean the other.

2. The reason she's fat is *because* she eats too much. *RIGHT*.

Those English teachers who are still bravely attempting to make their students say "The reason . . . is *that*" instead of the popular and perfectly logical "The reason . . . is *because*" are, I submit, waging a losing battle. The teachers base their argument on an involved grammatical abracadabra about copulative verbs taking noun, not adverbial, clauses; and the students (even the few who may understand what all this means) go out into the world armed with this precept only to find that adults whose wisdom and respectability are beyond question write and say "The reason . . . is *because*" more often than not. I leave it to you to imagine the confusion that results from this discrepancy between theory and practice.

Writing in a recent issue of *College English*, Professor

Russell Thomas, a member of the Committee on Current English Usage of the National Council of Teachers of English, reports: "The evidence which I have gathered shows that 'The reason . . . is *because*' type of sentence has become established as good colloquial and literary English."

3. It's *a phenomena*, that's what it is! *WRONG*.

*Phenomena* is one of the many paradoxes in the English language—it looks and sounds like a singular word, but it is completely and definitely plural, and is so treated in good usage. We may say, admiringly, "It's *a phenomenon*, that's what it is!" but we restrict the form *phenomena* to plural patterns, such as "*Those phenomena are* difficult to explain." *Criteria*, another paradox, has similar forms: *one criterion, many criteria*. However, *data* and *insignia* have crossed the line; though strictly plural, they are now widely used as singulars, probably because their true singular forms, *datum* and *insigne*, are so rarely heard.

4. Measles *is* catching. *RIGHT*.

You can't always judge by appearances: *Phenomena* and *criteria* look singular; they're plural. *Measles* looks, plural; it's singular. Obviously, you cannot have one *measle*, and since *measles* refers to a single disease, it is correctly used with *is*. Likewise *mumps, rickets, shingles*, and other such interesting diseases that end in *s*.

5. Mathematics *are* a fascinating subject. *WRONG*.

*Mathematics*, though it perversely ends in *s*, is singular; it is *one* science, just as *measles* is *one* disease. Therefore, mathematics *is* a fascinating subject. However, when the word is used as other than the name of a science, it is usually plural as in "Let's figure the example again—I think your mathematics *are* wrong somewhere."

6. *Due to* a bad cold, he stayed home. *RIGHT*.

"This use of *due to*," says Margaret M. Bryant, Professor of English at Brooklyn College, "developed in the 17th century and has been constantly employed ever since, not only popularly, but also by magazine and editorial writers, as well as by authors of great distinction, among whom we may mention John Galsworthy."

If you have any friends of pedantic inclination, they will raise their eyebrows in shocked disapproval whenever you say *due to* where they would prefer *owing to* or *because of*, but I suggest that you stand your ground. You have wide authority on your side.

7. Please *try and* come early. *RIGHT*.

Here is a perfect example of how our language sometimes blithely ignores the restrictions placed upon it by academic grammar. (The strict rule requires *to* in place of *and*.) Such giants of English literature as John Milton, Samuel Johnson, George Eliot, and Matthew Arnold frequently used *try and* in their writing—isn't it, then, a bit stuffy to claim, as the purists do, that you and I are speaking bad English if we use it in our everyday conversation?

I wonder how these purists would react to the following bit of typical dialogue between two belligerent motorists: "I have a good mind to punch you right in the nose!" "Oh, yeah? Well, just try *and!*" Would they suggest that the second speaker, in the heat of argument, remember the rules of formal grammar and say "Well, just try *to*"?

8. She's much older than *me*. *WRONG*.

"It's *me*" is good English—it has been sanctified by educated usage. "Older than *me*," however, has received no such sanction. *I* is the preferred pronoun in this type of construction since the complete sentence is "She's much older than I *am*." Similarly, you're richer than *she* (is), I can drink more Scotch than *he* (can), they're smarter than *we* (are), and we eat more than *they* (do). If this is a little on the confusing side, you'll agree with the well-known humorist, Stephen Leacock, who said, "English pronouns are a disorderly and drunken lot. We no sooner straighten them up on one side than they fall over on the other."

9. Don't you envy her *luxurious* black hair? *WRONG.*

If her hair is truly *luxurious*, you have nothing to envy—it's a wig. Anything *luxurious* is man-made and can be bought in the open market place. If the black hair of the young lady in question is a rich, natural growth, call it *luxuriant*.

# *Thirtieth Day*

## JUST FOR FUN (VI)

### *I. ARE YOU QUICK WITH WORDS?*

Words are dealt with at varying rates—an average reader can cover 250–300 a minute; a speaker can utter about 200 a minute without rushing; a good typist cruises along at more than 60 a minute once she hits her stride; and without undue haste most people can write about 25 a minute in legible longhand.

But how fast can you *think* of words? Here is a short test of the speed of your verbal responses. You will find below 40 simple words—and your problems is to think of, and write in the appropriate space, a synonym for each beginning with the letters *la*. (For example, the answer to No. 1 is *lather*.) The idea is to get through all 40 as rapidly as possible.

This is not a test of your vocabulary, as every response required is a common word used in everyday conversation, but rather a measurement of the time you take to react to a verbal stimulus. Grab a pen or pencil, and either time yourself or have someone time you, using a timepiece with a second hand. Ready? *GO.*

1. foam     _____
2. put     _____
3. big     _____
4. final     _____
5. crippled     _____
6. work     _____

| 7. legal | _____ | 24. spear | _____ |
| 8. girl | _____ | 25. path | _____ |
| 9. pond | _____ | 26. nonprofessional | _____ |
| 10. den | _____ | 27. thickness | _____ |
| 11. ticket | _____ | 28. attorney | _____ |
| 12. prank | _____ | 29. avalanche | _____ |
| 13. spoon | _____ | 30. thievery | _____ |
| 14. lock | _____ | 31. slothful | _____ |
| 15. speech | _____ | 32. enduring | _____ |
| 16. maze | _____ | 33. principle | _____ |
| 17. absence | _____ | 34. whip | _____ |
| 18. lasso | _____ | 35. funny | _____ |
| 19. regret | _____ | 36. extravagant | _____ |
| 20. dull | _____ | 37. wash | _____ |
| 21. cupboard | _____ | 38. praise | _____ |
| 22. boy | _____ | 39. descend | _____ |
| 23. loose | _____ | 40. slim | _____ |

KEY: 1–lather, 2–lay (or laid), 3–large, 4–last, 5–lame, 6–labor, 7–lawful, 8–lass (or lassie), 9–lake (or lagoon), 10–lair, 11–label, 12–lark, 13–ladle, 14–latch, 15–language, 16–labyrinth, 17–lack, 18–lariat, 19–lament (or lamentation), 20–lackluster, 21–larder, 22–lad, 23–lax, 24–lance, 25–lane, 26–lay (or laic or laical), 27–layer, 28–lawyer, 29–landslide, 30–larceny, 31–lazy, 32–lasting, 33–law, 34–lash, 35–laughable, 36–lavish, 37–launder (or lave), 38–laud (or laudation), 39–land, 40–lank (or lanky).

*Speed Chart:*

4½–5 minutes—SLOW
4–4½ minutes—AVERAGE
3¼–4 minutes—ABOVE AVERAGE
2½–3½ minutes—SUPERIOR
Under 2½ minutes—PHENOMENAL

Your score is valid if you have 35 or more correct answers.

## II. THEY DON'T SOUND THE WAY THEY LOOK

Many English words are not pronounced the way they're spelled. For example, look at these:

*Pronounced*

| | |
|---|---|
| quay (an artificial wharf) | KEE |
| solder (a metal used to join other metals) | SOD′-ər |
| victuals (food) | VIT′-əlz |
| slough (a swamp) | SLOO |
| phthisic (tuberculosis) | TIZ′-ək |
| Sioux (an Indian tribe) | SOO |
| viscount (title of honor) | VY′-kount |
| colonel (army officer) | KER′-nəl |
| fjord (inlet of the sea) | FYORD |
| imbroglio (complicated situation) | im-BRŌL′-yō |

## III. JOG YOUR VOCABULARY

Here are brief definitions of 10 common English verbs that end in *-ate*. You probably know them all. But allowing yourself only two minutes, how many can you think of before time runs out?

1. to make easier _____ate
2. to tell _____ate
3. to chew _____ate
4. to speed up _____ate
5. to free _____ate
6. to make impure _____ate
7. to dig _____ate
8. to remove by surgery _____ate
9. to ruin _____ate
10. to make up for _____ate

KEY:   1—facilitate, 2—relate, 3—masticate, 4—accelerate, 5—liberate, 6—adulterate, 7—excavate, 8—amputate, 9—devastate, 10—compensate.


## IV. TEST YOUR VERBAL SPEED

Do you have a good, strong, *responsive* vocabulary? Is it easy for you to pull words out of the deep recesses of your mind on a second's notice? Are you able to react with great speed upon exposure to certain verbal stimuli?

You can answer all these questions in ten minutes or less. In each of the tests to follow, read the instructions carefully, analyze the sample questions and answers so that you're sure you know what will be required of you, and then allow yourself exactly two minutes to complete each test.

Your verbal speed is excellent if you can write eight or more correct answers in each test before time is called.

Take as long as you wish to read the directions and analyze the samples; start timing only when you've actually begun the test. You get 120 seconds on each complete group—that's an average of twelve seconds per item, for recognizing the stimulus, reacting to it, and writing down your answer. It's no cinch—do you think you can do it?

**Test 1**

*Instructions:* Write a word beginning with letter *K* to satisfy each definition. Samples:

| Definition | Answer |
|---|---|
| an insect | katydid |
| Eskimo canoe | kayak |

| Definition | | Your Answer |
|---|---|---|
| 1. German ruler | 1. | k_____ |
| 2. animal | 2. | k_____ |

| | |
|---|---|
| 3. sovereign | 3. k_____ |
| 4. a rascal | 4. k_____ |
| 5. a horseman | 5. k_____ |
| 6. to weave | 6. k_____ |
| 7. Mohammedan Bible | 7. k_____ |
| 8. wisdom | 8. k_____ |
| 9. doghouse | 9. k_____ |
| 10. color | 10. k_____ |

## Test 2

*Instructions:* Write a word that fits each definition and which ends in the letters *-ential*. The initial letter is supplied to speed your reaction. Samples:

| *Definition* | *Answer* |
|---|---|
| pertaining to the highest elective office in this country | presidential |
| fortunate | providential |

| *Definition* | *Your Answer* |
|---|---|
| 1. private secret | c_____ential |
| 2. showing regard for another's wishes; respectful | d_____ential |
| 3. necessary | e_____ential |
| 4. of no great importance; trivial | i_____ential |
| 5. possessing power or effect | i_____ential |
| 6. pertaining to contagious disease or plagues | p_____ential |
| 7. possible, though not yet actual | p_____ential |
| 8. showing favor | p_____ential |
| 9. connected with living abodes | r_____ential |
| 10. rushing, overwhelming, like a rapid stream | t_____ential |

## Test 3

*Instructions:* Write a word having the same meaning as each key word and starting with the letters *va-*. Samples:

| Key Word | Answer |
|---|---|
| a variety show | vaudeville |
| residence of the Pope | Vatican |

| | Key Word | Your Answer |
|---|---|---|
| 1. | empty | va_____ |
| 2. | wanderer | va_____ |
| 3. | conceited | va_____ |
| 4. | man–servant | va_____ |
| 5. | courage | va_____ |
| 6. | disappear | va_____ |
| 7. | conquer | va_____ |
| 8. | change | va_____ |
| 9. | a safe | va_____ |
| 10. | worthwhile | va_____ |

## Test 4

*Instructions:* Write a word *opposite* in meaning to the key word and starting with the letter *w*. Samples:

| Key Word | Answer |
|---|---|
| outside | within |
| summer | winter |

| | Key Word | Your Answer |
|---|---|---|
| 1. | sleep | w_____ |
| 2. | peace | w_____ |
| 3. | cold | w_____ |
| 4. | careless | w_____ |
| 5. | conserve | w_____ |

6. strong          w_____
7. poverty       w_____
8. ill                w_____
9. part, portion    w_____
10. foolishness     w_____

## Test 5

*Instructions:* Each of the following nouns has an adjective form, entirely different from it in appearance and sound. Write the adjective which starts with the given letter. Samples:

| Noun | Adjective |
|------|-----------|
| hand | manual |
| moon | lunar |

| | Noun | Adjective |
|---|------|-----------|
| 1. | year | a_____ |
| 2. | body | a_____ |
| 3. | king | r_____ |
| 4. | barber | t_____ |
| 5. | tooth | d_____ |
| 6. | foot | p_____ |
| 7. | tree | a_____ |
| 8. | doctor | m_____ |
| 9. | mouth | o_____ |
| 10. | church | e_____ |

KEY

*Test 1:* 1–Kaiser, 2–kangaroo, koala, 3–king, 4–knave, 5–knight, 6–knit, knot, 7–Koran, 8–knowledge, 9–kennel, 10–khaki.

*Test 2:* 1–confidential, 2–deferential, 3–essential, 4–inconsequential, 5–influential, 6–pestilential, 7–potential, 8–preferential, 9–residential, 10–torrential.

*Test 3:*   1—vacant, vapid, vacuous; 2—vagabond, vagrant; 3—vain; 4—valet; 5—valor; 6—vanish; 7—vanquish; 8—vary, variety; 9—vault; 10—valuable.

*Test 4:*   1—wake, 2—war, 3—warm, 4—wary, watchful, watching, wily; 5—waste; 6—weak; 7—wealth; 8—well; 9—whole; 10—wisdom, wit.

*Test 5:*   1—annual, 2—anatomical, 3—royal *or* regal, 4—tonsorial, 5—dental, 6—pedal, podiatric, *or* podial, 7—arboreal, 8—medical, 9—oral, 10—ecclesiastic *or* ecclesiastical.